ARE YOU REALLY WAITING: On God's Promise for a Divine Spouse?

ARE YOU REALLY WAITING: On God's Promise
for a Divine Spouse?

Prophetess Evangelist Fern Yvette Harris, PhD

All Scripture quotations are from the King James Version of the Bible.

All definitions marked (MWCD) are from the Merriam-Webster collegiate dictionary®, (11th ed.), (1995). Spring-field, MA: Merriam-Webster.

All Hebrew and Greek definitions marked (S.C.) are from The New Strong's Exhaustive Concordance of the Bible, Copyright © 1990 by Thomas Nelson Publishers

All definitions marked (Vines) are from the Vine's Complete Expository Dictionary of Old and New Testament Words, Copyright © 1985, by Thomas Nelson Publishers

"Are You Really Waiting: *On God's Promise for a Divine Spouse?*" by Prophetess Fern Yvette Harris, PhD

Cover illustration inspired by the Holy Ghost: Prophetess Fern Yvette Harris, PhD

Published by: Prophetess Evangelist Fern Yvette Harris, PhD
4980 S. Alma School Road
Ste. A2, #259
Chandler, AZ 85248
www.ATcicJMinistries.org

ISBN 979-8-9858790-0-1
Copyright © 2022 by Dr. Fern Yvette Harris
Printed in the United States of America

2nd Edition

This book is dedicated to all the single Christian women who struggle with waiting on a divine connection. You don't have to look for him, he will find you!

"Whoso findeth a wife findeth a good thing, and obtaineth favour of the Lord."

Proverbs 18:22

TABLE OF CONTENTS

PREFACE

In the Body of Christ, many women are waiting for God to send them a husband. However, the truth is many of the husbands had come and gone because the women failed to discern who he was when he arrived. When your divine connection comes, it is possible that you may be more involved in a fantasy about some other man and will not be ready to receive your blessing. Or you may fail to prepare yourself spiritually and will not be able to hear clearly from the Lord about which one is the right one.

You may also fail in spiritual strength and will not stand amid all the voices of people who will try to tell you what to do and what decision to make. This book will open your eyes to the tricks the adversary uses against women in the Church and what to do about it.

ACKNOWLEDGEMENTS

I would like to thank Jesus Christ, my Lord, and Savior, for trusting me with the experiences in this book, for being ever so faithful to me, and for the deliverance and maturity that came forth because of each divinely orchestrated event. Lord, you never let me down.

To my husband, Michealangelo Harris, the Lord's true Apostle Prophet: Sweetie, you've always been there with encouraging and reassuring words. Thanks for encouraging me to be all the Lord chose me to be. Thank you for your input concerning the title and cover work of this book.

I would like to honor my late mom-in-law, Lillie Harris, for being there in hard times. I often thanked her for loving me when I didn't deserve it. I'll see her in the rapture.

To Christopher and Chrison: Your love stayed the same. Thank You for your unfailing unconditional love. I am thankful the Lord chose me to be your mother. I will always love you. Keep striving to please and obey God and not man, Acts 5:29.

To my big sister Pamela: It was just as hard for you as for me during this trial. You knew what the Lord was doing because you were neutral. Your heart toward me was right, so the Lord was able to reveal the truth to you, even though others thought you were wrong. I was able to hold on to what the Lord was saying to me because of your many prayers. Thanks for being there in the spirit realm. I love you dearly.

To my brother Cedric who loved my sons and me regardless of what others said, you've been taking care of me since I was a little girl. You have a special place in my heart.

To my sister Tracey: Thanks for staying neutral and loving me anyway. I love you always.

To Prophetess Sherry Nickerson: What an accurate word you had in your mouth for my life. You encouraged me in ways you didn't know. I'm thankful to have had someone like you at my lowest point in life.

To all the ATcicJ Ministries disciples, I love you all. Thanks for your support.

INTRODUCTION

The purpose of this book is to speak to my sisters in the Body of Christ about waiting on God's promise for a spouse. I had been through many rocky relationships in my life, and when I came to Christ, I fell in love with Him. From the beginning, He truly has been my all in all. I had no desire to pursue a relationship with or date anyone except the man I believed God would later place in my life to be my husband.

Because I didn't know anything about Christianity or being saved, I had a burning desire to study the Word. I talked to God often and was fascinated with understanding His principles for living. With a desire to truly learn who Christ is and what being a Christian is all about, I left my old life behind completely, including some family and friends, and was on a life-changing experience with God.

I received salvation in a ministry that was Holy Spirit-led. The Bishop encouraged us to read the Word of God for ourselves and to be obedient to the Lord's voice. He told us that we must live holy and avoid the appearance of evil; he also discouraged hypocrisy. I took my Bishop at his word and did all I could to live the Word of God. This included waiting for a spouse.

After being saved for some time, I was surprised to see many happily married couples in the Church. I noticed that the couples worked together on the same auxiliaries in the ministry. I also noticed that there were lots of children and families together! Wow, it was new for me to see both parents raising their children.

Also, I found out that many of the couples were happily married for an extended period. This was amazing because everyone I knew in my old life was separated, divorced, or never married. It was more common to have children out of wedlock than to have children within the marriage covenant. I've always loved seeing other people in love, and this was amazing. I began to hope that God would send that right man into my life and that our marriage would be a happy one.

Some time went on, and I realized that the sisters were supposed to wait for God to send the man into our life. I began to understand Scriptures like Proverbs 18:22, *"Whoso findeth a wife findeth a good thing, and obtaineth favor of the Lord."* So, with this Scripture in mind, I understood that my job was to wait! I set my mind, soul, spirit, and BODY to do just that. Wait!

Chapter 1

Why Are You Still Single?

"Therefore if any man be in Christ, he is a new creature: old things are passed away; behold, all things are become new."

2nd Corinthians 5:17

CHAPTER 1: WHY ARE YOU STILL SINGLE?

I grew up in Michigan, the third eldest of seven children. My parents were the closest example of a marriage that I can remember. By the time I was 14 years old, they were pending divorce. After my parent's divorce, my desire to be married diminished as I grew into adulthood.

As a teenager, I was in an abusive relationship wherein I started having sex. I saw many of my family members go through difficult marriages and common-law relationships. The common theme in each situation was violence, adultery, fornication, and distrust. Some of the women in these situations began to say, "I don't need a man; I can do bad all by myself," and I believed them. From my perspective, marriage was gloom and doom.

At 30 years of age, I received Christ as my Lord and Savior. My life began to change immediately. Shortly after receiving salvation, the untimely deaths of one of my brothers and a co-worker drove me to a closer walk with the Lord. I disciplined myself to rise at 5 A.M. to praise, worship, pray, and study the Word of God before I started my workday. After work, I repeated my morning routine for hours on days I didn't have Church. I stopped watching television for three years to dedicate my extra time to seeking the Lord.

During these three years, the Lord began to prepare me for the future had for me; however, I didn't know it. I received deliverance in many areas of my life, and others noticed the tremendous changes the Lord was doing in me. After about five years into my walk with Jesus, I thought I was delivered from my past.

The truth was there were still so many areas of my life that I needed to face concerning men and respecting authority, especially what I perceived as an abusive authority. I was so messed up that I could not discern what abuse really was. I thought if I couldn't get my way, it was abuse. If a man took charge, I saw him as controlling and abusive. Now mind you, in the Church setting, I was taught that the man was supposed to take charge. However, outside of the Church, I had a lot of difficulties respecting men in authority.

I can think back to several times in my life when the Lord was trying to get my attention concerning this weakness in my character, and my response would be aggression. I would feel convicted afterward, ask the person to forgive me, and for a short while, I would see some change. However, most of the time, I was truly afraid to look deeply at this area of my character, so I ignored it, hoping it would go away. Besides, my life was so busy that I didn't have time to deal with it, yet it was hindering me from truly moving forward.

At other times I would see this negative area as something positive in my character. I saw myself as taking a stand against men who were trying to humiliate me. Men saw in my character the virtues of a man and not a woman. I thought I was strong by not allowing anyone to use a stern tone with me or challenge my obscure way of thinking. I thought the Lord was with me as I took a stand against those in authority over me. On the contrary, I wasn't taking a stand at all. I was refusing to humble myself. The more I refused, the more I found myself in conflict with authority.

I had problems at work with male bosses, at Church with men in authority, in the family respecting my uncles, brothers, and cousins, and they were much older than me. I was operating in ignorance, not perceiving what was required in the Word of God in this area of my life.

This was a problem buried deep down in my soul. I learned to cover it up with prayer when I needed to. Sometimes I would find myself meditating on this area of my character, yet never genuinely asking the Lord for help in dealing with it. Then when stress or unpredictable situations would occur, the truth would seep out of my character again. It wasn't until 9 ½ years after receiving salvation, that I began to understand what was really going on with me.

The truth was I was afraid of having a husband, especially one who would walk in the Word and expect obedience and respect. Any man in authority would soon know the truth about me if he got too close. I was one unstable woman when it came to men. I would either be too shy, or I was having outbursts.

You may wonder what this has to do with waiting on a spouse. Well, it has everything to do with it because the very things I would not humble myself to and let go of before my divine connection came were the same things I had to face once he arrived. He was the only one that would love me enough to stay while God took me through the process of deliverance. This was the most challenging thing I ever had to face. There were times when he wondered if I was the one for him because I was having so many outbursts. Also, if you don't get cleaned up before your spouse comes, you will marry what you are spiritually.

I was angry because I felt men misunderstood my strength. I was defensive toward men who would speak the truth because I grew up with men who often abused women and children. So, I formed many negative stereotypes about men. It was rare when a man could tell me something, and I would listen with no resistance.

I was bitter because my parents were divorced, and it affected me in many ways that I did not know. For example, I would get depressed at the same time every year and didn't realize, until I was 33 years old, that it was connected to my parent's divorce. I asked the Lord why this was happening every year, and He showed me the breach in my parent's marriage. The Lord healed me of this, yet I still had issues with men.

I was headstrong and extremely strong-willed because all the women in my family were this way. The men in my family didn't like that the women in the family were aggressive and contentious, and they could do nothing about it. After all, this had gone on for generations.

None of the women took the time to reflect on why they didn't have husbands. Either they didn't marry, were separated, or divorced. I watched three generations of women without husbands, and two generations of women have babies out of wedlock or frequent the abortion clinics. I watched women trick their husbands and men friends by claiming other men's children were theirs. I heard the women emphasize and reemphasize men were dogs. This was normal in my family, and no one told me it was wrong. I became a lot of what I watched and heard.

I was full of pride and arrogance and often promised myself I would do whatever it took to not let a man ruin or run my life. I made a vow to myself and tried desperately to keep it; I did not marry. People always asked me why I wasn't married, and I would say, "No one ever asked me." This was because I was an uncontrollable raging woman. Prior to salvation, I often said I didn't need a man for anything but sex.

I was full of fear and tried to hide the truth that the Lord had given me a desire to be married deep down on the inside, and I was afraid of being hurt. I was afraid of submitting to someone stronger than me, and I continually tried to manipulate men emotionally to get my way. I would throw temper tantrums often to get attention or burst into crying spells like a two-year-old child. Some of the women in my family had mastered this and used it to often manipulate everyone into getting what they needed.

Once, I even got to a place where I began to physically abuse a man I was with because I was hurt about a previous relationship. When I was a teenager, I told my mother I desired to have children; however, I didn't desire a husband. I was afraid of being trapped with a man that would mistreat my children and me. I thought marriage was too final. So, my words to my mother began to come to fruition while in college. I became pregnant during my second year and had no thoughts of marriage. When my first child was six weeks old, I received a marriage offer but I said no. I railed on him so badly that it broke his spirit. That relationship ended after five years and two children. Even after I was saved, I taught my sons that they didn't need a dad. I Thank God we all came to know that that is not true. All children need a dad.

The bottom line is, when I was in the world, I had a gross misunderstanding of who I really was. I thought because I was not with more than one partner at a time, didn't steal men's money, didn't lie about the true identity of my children's biological dad, didn't drink alcohol or do drugs, I was special, not even considering that fornication is a sin. I thought I was better than other women. I didn't say it, but unconsciously this was how I carried myself. The truth was just the opposite, and now I'm a baby saint and desire a husband. I was ready for what God had for me, yeah Right!

Chapter 2

I Know Who My Husband Is

"Then when lust have conceived, it bringeth forth sin: and sin, when it is finished, bringeth forth death. Do not err, my beloved brethren. Every good gift and every perfect gift is from above, and cometh down from the Father of lights, with whom is no variableness, neither shadow of turning."

James 1:15-17

CHAPTER 2: I KNOW WHO MY HUSBAND IS

Like many immature sisters in the Body of Christ, of all ages, the adversary tricked me into thinking that a certain man in the Church was my husband. It was about 8 months into my salvation walk, and this trick lasted for over a year. The thing that was interesting about this particular deception was that I didn't see this person as someone who would be my spouse. I didn't feel attracted to him in any way. However, I did notice that he was a man of wisdom; so, I accepted that he could be the one. I didn't know at that time that God doesn't force people to be together. Really! I didn't know much of anything about Christian relationships, just the testimonies of other people.

The deception started when I began having dreams about his personal life, and I began to intercede and pray for him daily. I didn't have feelings or thoughts of lust, nor did I ever approach or pursue him in any way. However, I did come to desire his attention. After a long time had gone by and he did not show any interest in me, I found myself getting angry. I couldn't understand why he would not ask me out on a date. Now, remember, I was not ready for a relationship, especially not marriage, and I didn't know it. I thought I could overcome the way I was raised with a positive Christian attitude.

13

During this time, I realized that many sisters thought they knew who their husbands were; they would pursue the man and do things to get his attention, only to end up hurt and bitter at the end when he chose someone else. No matter how many warnings the overseer and his wife gave the single sisters, the devil said to me, "Yeah, but it's not like that with you. This is different. Someone has to be his wife." Also, there were several others who were close to me who had dreams of me with this person. It's all a part of the adversary's plan to get the sister's mind off Jesus and onto some man, the wrong man!

When I found out that he wasn't the one, I felt relieved. I wasn't angry; I was relieved! Then I started hearing more and more that this was happening to the single brothers in the Church. Dozens of women thought that the same man was to be their husband. It was sickening! I felt righteous indignation because the adversary was tricking so many women. Not only did I decide not to date, but I also made sure not to even think that someone could possibly be my mate. I decided that the man would have to come to me first. I asked the Lord not to allow me to have any dreams of weddings, men in the

Church, etc. Although I was young in Christ, I did not like being tricked.

I came to understand that the dreams I had were the Lord's way of leading me to pray for him because he was a leader in the Church fighting his own personal battles. The Lord was also grooming me to be an intercessor. God showed me things concerning him that later I found out were true. However, he was not the man destined to be my husband.

When I began to pray for him aloud, the adversary knew I started having dreams and began to give me dreams that he was watching me with interest. I even had a dream that he gave me an engagement ring. I never found out whether he was genuinely interested or not because I never asked him, but after the first publication of this book, the Lord Jesus let me know that he was not the one ordained for me. It was one big misunderstanding and a dangerous trick of the adversary. The Bible declares: *"My people are destroyed for lack of knowledge:" (Hosea 4:6a).*

Shortly after the truth came out, I received a phone call from one of the sisters in the Church who also thought this person was my husband. She said, "Aren't you upset about all those prayers you sent up for him?" I said, "No!" The prayers I prayed were sincere and were not contingent on him being my husband. I prayed the will of God into this person's life. It didn't bother me one bit. Besides, I knew that because of my prayers, someone would, one day, pray for me and my marriage. *"Be not deceived; God is not mocked: for whatsoever a man soweth, that shall he also reap" (Galatians 6:7).*

It was amazing that the dreams stopped after the truth came out that he was dating someone else! Yet other sisters continued to humiliate themselves by giving brothers cards with money, notes with their phone numbers, and letters. Some have even plainly invited men in the Church to their apartments. Some even confronted men who were dating another woman because they felt he should be dating them.

I've seen two women engaged to the same man in a two-month period. He marries the latter sister, and the marriage ends in disaster just a few months later. The last I heard, this man lost his mind, literally! I believe the Lord spared me much heartache because of my sincerity in desiring to know and operate in the truth. *"Blessed are they which do hunger and thirst after righteousness: for they shall be filled" (Matthew 5:6).*

My word of warning to all the sisters who desire a husband! Every time a man comes to the Church that looks like the man you described to the Lord, don't lose your senses and start pursuing him; it doesn't mean he is your husband. Every time you meet a nice Christian man, it doesn't mean he is the one. I cannot count the number of single Christian women who see my husband in a store, and they are hoping he is the one for them. When they find out he is already married, they have an attitude.

Listen, when you meet a Christian man, he may be a good man, but it doesn't mean he's YOUR man. Every time you have a dream or see a man looking at you in Church, it doesn't mean he is your dream man. Just because you are a great worshipper and have awesome spiritual gifts or a beautiful singing voice, it doesn't mean you're going to get a husband. You can't praise God and make him give you a husband who is not ordained for you!

The bottom line is the Lord decides who gets a husband. The Lord decides how your husband will look and the manner of his heart. You just need to be open to receive whom God has for you. Whether you get married or not will depend on the work the Lord has for your husband and you to do and not the work you have for a husband;

sisters, you know the saying, "I can't wait until I get married so he can pay the bills."

Listen, don't let the enemy trick you. STOP looking and wait on God! When your husband comes, you are going to know it. You will not have to do anything to entice him or lead him on before he notices other women. You will not have to drop a handkerchief or a book to see if he notices and picks it up. Stop playing games, and the game will stop being played on you!

Sisters, when you stop playing games, you will no longer believe the line, "The Lord said I'm your husband." Brothers, how is it in one month you are saying, "The Lord said you are my wife," and then three months go by and you get to know her, then you say, "It's not going to work?" Don't you think the Lord knew her before you approached her? Stop playing games and really put your trust in the Lord and wait for Him to show you your wife. I prayed and asked God not to allow my husband to approach me that way, and he didn't.

I knew a sister in the Church who dated several guys who told her, "God said you are my wife." Brother, why are you lying on God? Aren't you afraid of giving an account to God for tricking and taking advantage of His children? *"So then every one of us shall give*

18

account of himself to God" (Romans 14:12). The Lord let me know that when a man says that to a woman, and it is really the Lord, the Lord is saying for that single sister to be married to Him. They should be consecrating themselves to the Lord and not be thinking about being married. They are not ready to be anybody's wife! Leave that sister alone and give her time to unload her old baggage!

Brother, God will defend every woman you trick and defraud. *"That no man go beyond and defraud his brother in any matter: because that the Lord is the avenger of all such, as we also have forewarned you and testified" (1st Thessalonians 4:6).* In this case, defraud in the Greek (S.C. 4122), means to be covetous, to over-reach, get an advantage, and make a gain.

Ladies, once the games cease, the mind games cease, and you will make room for a real, Godly man to come into your life. Besides, what Godly man desires to marry a woman who had already dated every other available brother in the ministry before he got there? Can you imagine what the other brothers will say to him about you? It won't be good.

Men are naturally competitive by nature. It doesn't change because they are saved. Imagine your fiancé getting excited about showing you off to his friends, but his friends (the other brothers in the Church) already know what you are like. They have already dated you and your children. They know your attitude, what turns you on and off. They know whether you can cook or not. They know whether you clean at home or not. They know whether you are really saved! They know your nasty attitude, so your fiancé can't brag. He can't even hide your flaws because the other brothers already know. You can't be his trophy because you have already been on everyone else's shelf.

What is it that you don't desire your new fiancé to know? These men may tell him. And the other sisters are going to tell your secrets too because some of them are still playing games. They covet your man, and you have given them enough ammunition to get him. When my husband arrived, there was nothing anyone could tell him about me because I had not dated anyone. This allowed us to get to know each other and build a trusting relationship. There was no web of lies told by other people that we had to untangle.

Many folks are playing more games in the Church than in the world. It's clear that single, Godly men in the Church are scarce, so when one arrives, oftentimes, several sisters are hoping he's there for her. He's like fresh meat on the butcher's block. And when you are desperate, your flesh will do anything to get and keep that man, even if you know the truth about him. The carnal nature (flesh) is not strong but weak, and there is no good thing in it. If a woman is truly consecrated, she will not be CHASING MEN. And a truly spiritual woman that is waiting on God will not settle for, nor marry, a carnal man, no matter how long she has waited. *"For I know that in me (that is, in my flesh,) dwelleth no good thing: for to will is present with me; but how to perform that which is good I find not" (Romans 7:18).*

Sisters, the men that date several women in the Church or date the sisters who have dated several other brothers in the Church, have one thing on their mind, and it's not marriage. They want to satisfy their flesh. Once they get their flesh fed, they are going to drop you like a hot iron, have a feeling of worldly sorrow, and run to the next unsuspecting sister they can trick. *"For godly sorrow worketh repentance to salvation not to be repented of"* but the sorrow of the *world worketh death" (2nd Corinthians 7:10).*

And sweetie, you will be left with another soul tie that brings heartache, anger, emotional trauma, bitterness, hatred toward men, shame, unforgivingness, regret, sorrow, sexually transmitted diseases,

21

abortions, or possibly a baby. These are only some of the things you will have to be delivered from all over again.

"For this is the will of God, even your sanctification, that ye should abstain from fornication: That every one of you should know how to possess his vessel in sanctification and honour; Not in the lust of concupiscence (coveting, abnormal desire, lust), even as the Gentiles which know not God: . . . For God hath not called us to uncleanness, but unto holiness" (1st Thessalonians 4:3-5, 7).

Ladies, understand that there is something in you that draws these men to you or you to them. It declares in James 1:14, *"But every man is tempted when he is drawn away of his own lust, and enticed."* So, make up in your mind right now that the man you are eyeing is not your husband. If he were the one, he would know about it. If he were the one, he would have already sincerely approached you. However, if he doesn't know, you have to wait until he does. Once he knows, he will ask permission of his spiritual leaders first. By involving the leaders of the Church, there will be consequences if he is playing a game. Also, they can warn you if he is a womanizer.

You can't afford to think you are the exception. When you think you are the exception to the rule, you open a bigger door for the adversary to trick you further. Jesus could be talking to you to help you get out of the situation, and you will think it's the devil keeping you from a blessing. When you refuse to listen to God or can't discern the truth, you will become infatuated with the lie. It becomes who you are and what you live for. It will be the reason you go to Church. This is one clue that your thinking is not God.

This is why I believe so many sisters are not married in the Church. They are already married to a fantasy. The Lord can't send the true man he has for you because you are in lust with someone else or you are married to your children to a degree where a husband can't be received.

Chapter 3

Me and My Stuff

"And he said unto them, Take heed, and beware of covetousness: for a man's life consisteth not in the abundance of the things which he possesseth."

Luke 12:15

CHAPTER 3: ME & MY STUFF

From my perspective, women in America are dominating the education arena, the workplace, and the home. We have become examples in our community. Women are more likely to attend college, get white-collar jobs before men in poorer communities, and run households single-handedly.

Women are city and county leaders, governors of states, members of Congress, high-ranking military personnel, and members of the president's cabinet. Women are athletes and spiritual leaders. Some women even claim to be Apostles, Prophets, and Bishops, even though this is contrary to the Word of God. We have increased in this world's goods and material possessions in abundance. There are not many places that women have not reached.

However, the one thing a woman can never be no matter what title she carries or what she achieves, and that is a <u>head</u> according to the Lord's standards. She may be in a leadership position; however, she is not a head from the Lord's perspective. She may have a title of captain, chief, commander, director, guide, master, but she will never be a head; that is true headship because it is something males are born with when the Lord sends them to Earth. A woman who has sons will be their guardian, but not their head.

When you look these words up in the (MWCD), they are listed as synonyms. They all basically mean the same thing, the one who is in charge. However, in Scripture, this is not so. According to Scripture, the opposite of head is follower or subordinate; this is the woman's place. I have nothing to say against women's independence, and I am not advocating male chauvinism. I believe the Lord has given women many unique gifts and abilities that He didn't give men. And I am not advocating women go back to only being "barefoot and pregnant" and never living up to their God-given potential.

I am advocating women tap into the true power the Lord will give them when they submit to their husbands. Not only will they be successful naturally, but they will also have power with God and discover they have a blessed and happy marriage. Women will find life more fulfilling when they find their rightful place in the Body of Christ instead of trying to stand in the place ordained for the man.

I believe men will be held to a greater level of accountability to the Lord for the state of his family, and this is not an account that women will desire to give when it's all said and done. The Lord requires more of men; standing before God and giving an account for one's actions will be a serious thing. The point I'm trying to make is that the woman is to be the subordinate, the follower of her husband. It becomes a problem when a woman allows her achievements to trick her into disrespecting her husband's God-given headship position.

"For the husband is the head of the wife, even as Christ is the head of the church: and he is the savior of the body" *(Ephesians 5:23)*. The Word of God declares that the head of the woman is her husband. This means no matter what position the woman will attain, she will always be subordinate to her husband. This means the CEO in the office is subordinate to her husband, who may be a mailman.

This truth hinders many women from having husbands because they do not desire to obey and submit. They believe their accomplishments give them the right to be in a place of authority over the man. Many women believe that the man is accountable to them because of the anointing on the woman's life. This is not true. It is not in the Lord's divine plan for a woman to rule over the man. Isaiah 3:12c-f declares, *"and women rule over them. O my people, they which lead thee cause thee to err, and destroy the way of thy paths."*

When a woman rules over her husband, she will cause the entire household to err.

This word submit means to subordinate, to obey, to be under obedience, put under, subdue unto, be or make subject to or unto, in subjection to or under, and to submit self unto. If you don't believe me, research Strong's Concordance (5293) under the words submit or subjection.

In the Merriam-Webster's Collegiate Dictionary submit means to lower, submit, to yield to governance or authority, to subject to a treatment, condition, or operation, to yield oneself to the authority or will of another: surrender, to permit oneself to be subjected to something, or to defer to or consent to abide by the opinion or authority of another. If you do not submit to your husband, you are not submitting to God, and if you are not submitting to God, your flesh is in control. Romans 8:8 declares, *"So then they that are in the flesh cannot please God."* I don't care how much you pray and how well you can prophesy; if you are not submitting to your husband, you are not pleasing God.

Stop misusing the Scripture that declares the husband and wife submit one to another. Apostle Paul was writing concerning the brethren in the Church, not the husband and wife. It declares in Ephesians 5:21-22, *"Submitting yourselves one to another in the fear of God. Wives, submit yourselves unto your own husbands, as unto the Lord."* Note, after Apostle Paul writes in verse 21 about submitting one to another, he immediately writes in verse 22, "**wives, submit yourselves unto your own husbands!**" It was as if he was bringing clarity because he knew some woman would misconstrue verse 21, and unfortunately, over time, men have joined in and agreed with the error.

Can you imagine a household where two people constantly submit to each other and no one has ultimate accountability or authority? It would be like two people trying to get into a building, and both are saying, "You first, no you first, no you first, no you first, no you first." No one would ever walk through the door. My husband told me, "Anything with two heads is a monster."

Your material wealth, career, or position does not make you. If you fall apart when the material wealth is taken away, you were nothing to begin with. When God gives husbands, He is looking at His daughters' hearts. If you desire to be married to have a boy toy in

31

the bedroom, you will not get a true man of God; if you marry, you will be hard-pressed to keep him.

Think about the divorce rate in the Body of Christ. It's just as high as the world's divorce rate. Why do you think that is? From the woman's side, we do not desire to submit. We play games with our husbands, "I can hear from God more than you or just as much as you, or God told me, so and so." Fill in the blanks, ladies. There are many women in the Church questioning what their husbands do. They question every decision he makes, thinking he's accountable to them, but the Word of God declares: **<u>Christ is his head!</u>** He will give an account to Christ for his actions.

If your heart is not right toward men and you are not willing to yield to the Lord's plan for marriage, you will not be getting a Godly husband. Instead, you may end up with a carnal man. He will be a man and not the promise from God. The promise of God will be the man the Lord sends according to His plan and purpose for your life. And it may require some waiting.

A true Godly man needs a woman who will walk in the Word. Not just some woman who has a nice face or shapely body. A real, Godly man desires a Godly woman first. He doesn't need a woman who cares more for her material possessions than she does for him or the work of God. A carnal (worldly, earthly-minded) woman will bail out on the marriage when times get hard or finances are few. This is evident by all the women who bail out of marriages when things do not go their way. Believe me, there is a season for prosperity and a season for famine. And a woman of vanity will not be able to stand in a season of famine.

"Lay not up for yourselves treasures upon earth, where moth and rust doth corrupt, and where thieves break through and steal: But lay up for yourselves treasures in heaven, where neither moth nor rust doth corrupt, and where thieves do not break through and steal: For where your treasure is, there will your heart be also" (Matthew 6:19-21).

So, just because you are a manager on your job does not mean you can lord it over your husband. I'm not talking about carnal men, even though the carnal husband should be obeyed. A woman with a carnal husband needs a lot more wisdom so he can be converted. And sisters, don't let your Pastor tell you that you don't have to listen to your unsaved husband. Yes, you do!! I'm not saying commit sin or do that which will displease the Lord. I'm saying don't you despise your husbands! You were the one who married him. Now that you are saved, don't act crazy and miss an opportunity for the Lord to save him. Just walk in the Word of God, use wisdom, and the Lord will bless you. *"Likewise, ye wives, be in subjection to your own husbands; that, if any obey not the Word, they also may without the word be won by the conversation of the wives" (1st Peter 3:1).*

One example of this was when I was saved less than two years and a woman came to our Church having just received salvation. Her husband was a good man, and he was not saved. She was spending all her time with the Church, and he started to get upset and shared his feelings with her. Since the Lord used me to welcome her to the Church, she shared this situation with me. I told her to make sure she spent time with her husband. I thought within myself, "A lot of women have been waiting a long time to be married; if he is good to you, you'd be crazy to mess that up."

A short time later, she told me he desired that she miss Church on New Year's Eve and spend that time with him. Since we sang in the choir together, she mentioned it to me, and I told her she should spend that time with her husband, who had already expressed that he did not desire to visit the Church that evening. She listened to me, and within a short time after, her husband received salvation and was faithful to the Lord.

God has ordained the man for the position of headship, and nothing and no one can change that. Even Christ's death on the cross did not put the woman in a position of authority over her husband. The woman is still considered the weaker vessel. She needs a covering to keep watch over her. Some women will not be saved without a husband to watch for their souls because many are rebellious, gossiping, hell raisers. And get this: If you are ordained to be married and you do not marry to avoid submitting, you are displeasing the Lord. And if you claim to be a believer that is not good. John 14:15 declares, *"If ye love me, keep my commandments."*

Apostle Paul said that he would not suffer the woman to teach or usurp authority over the man. He said that he did not suffer a woman to teach. I believe he said this because he knew the woman's nature. She is prone to lift herself above the man if given the opportunity, thereby operating in deception. *"Let the woman learn in silence with all subjection. But I suffer not a woman to teach, nor to usurp authority over the man, but to be in silence. For Adam was first formed, then Eve. And Adam was not deceived, but the woman being deceived was in the transgression" (1ˢᵗ Timothy 2:11-14).*

Let's face it, with all of our achievements, we still long for and need one thing, a husband who will love us. After we have our spiritual needs in order, after we have achieved what we desired in the natural, after the education, the career, the homes, the travels, the cars, and the business, we yearn for a husband. After we have reached the heavenlies with our prayers and worship, there is still the desire for the love of a true Godly husband. The Lord God made women this way.

I'm not talking about what the world calls love. Nowadays, people get a funny feeling in their lower parts and call it love. I mean true love as intended in the Word of God, the kind of love that cherishes and nurtures. The kind of love that is not contingent on what you have or what you can bring to the table. The love I'm talking about is not contingent on how you look or how great a reputation you have or only loves because of your spiritual or natural gifts. It is the love that the Lord requires of a man for a woman, his bride.

"Husbands, love your wives, even as Christ also loved the church, and gave himself for it; . . . So ought men to love their wives as their own bodies. He that loveth his wife loveth himself. For no man ever yet hated his own flesh; but nourisheth and cherisheth it, even as the Lord the church: . . . For this cause shall a man leave his father and mother, and shall be joined unto his wife, and they two shall be one flesh. This is a great mystery: but I speak concerning Christ and the church. Nevertheless let every one of you in particular so love his wife even as himself; and the wife see that she reverence her husband" (Ephesians 5:25, 28-29, 31-33).

Now, who honestly would trade that type of love for material possessions? Who would trade that type of love for loneliness? Who would trade that type of love for worldly power? Most women will never have this love as long as they are looking at their stuff and how men measure up to it. The Lord will not be thinking about your stuff when He decides to send a husband to you. He's thinking about the work the two of you can do together for His Kingdom. He's thinking about the Godly seed that the union will produce and how He can use this marriage to bless His Kingdom for generations.

More than likely, you have a preconceived idea of what he is supposed to be when he comes. It's possible that you may have achieved more than he has when he arrives. He may not have a college degree, business, or even own a home, and he is the man God is sending you. He may not measure up to the standards of your friends and family members, and they may try to convince you to let him go. And you may let him go because he doesn't measure up to your ideals, your Pastor's ideals, your natural daddy's ideals, etc.

Know for a surety that if you let him go, you will miss out on what God has for you and will <u>spend many years in the Church waiting</u> for something that will never happen because you have already missed your season for that ONE DIVINE CONNECTION. Many women have seen a vision of the plan for marriage the Lord has for them, but it is just a mirage. It is something you will only see and never have because you have already missed it.

"For my thoughts are not your thoughts, neither are your ways my ways, saith the Lord. For as the heavens are higher than the earth, so are my ways higher than your ways, and my thoughts than your thoughts" (Isaiah 55:8-9).

Think about this: The man of God, your spiritual leader, that you admire so much, where did he come from? Was it small beginnings? I'm talking about your Pastor, the same one who may tell you not to be with a man who has nothing, even though the Pastor came from nothing. If he is a true man of God, he had a small beginning too or is familiar with struggling. God does not have any superstars.

We, as women, have to see the potential in the divine connection the Lord sends us. You must seek God concerning what He is going to do in that man He sends you. Don't go by what anyone else has to say about him. Seek God for yourself. When God speaks, He will show you things others will not see in him. I often wonder about the many women in Churches who have missed their divine connection because they have listened to other people. Countless women in the Body of Christ have missed God and don't even know it. They are still waiting on someone who will never come.

Years ago, I heard a teaching series on marriage. The women were told to be careful about who they got involved with when getting married because some men "wanted a sponsor." This is the counsel we were given: we were told if we owned a home before we married, not to sell that home until we knew for sure that the marriage was going to work out. We were told not to have any shared bank accounts or credit cards in the beginning until we knew this person was not going to take us for our money. Let me tell you, if you go into a marriage with this type of distrust, you will have serious problems in your marriage.

What if the shoe was on the other foot and the woman had nothing? Would it be right for the man to say, "You can't be on my bank account or have any of my credit cards with your name on it?" How can she take care of business or shop with everything separated like that? Women, we would be the first to say, "That man is selfish, no good, and controlling."

Well, if the woman is doing it, then she gets to wear the same labels. If your material wealth is that important, then you should stay single. And the truth about marriage in Christ is we need to trust the Lord in our decisions. If the Lord is truly in it, there is no place for doing things the way the world does. I don't believe pre-nuptial agreements are of God. Before I received salvation, I had this same mindset of distrust. I was not going to have any man's name on anything I owned. Everything would be separate. I even had a problem with married women needing their husbands' permission to request a portion of profit-sharing money accumulated at the woman's job. Now that I am married, I find joy operating together with my husband as one.

Another major issue I had was the idea of giving up my maiden name. I was so wrapped up in my own identity and career that I was unwilling to accept a husband's last name if the Lord sent me one. I often pondered whether I would keep or hyphenate my last name so I could hold on to my identity as a single woman. The truth is a woman who keeps her maiden name or hyphenates her name is not truly one with the husband she has married.

I'm not speaking about certain nations where it is cultural for the woman to keep both family names; most of the women of these nations believe and operate in the principles of submission. I'm talking about a woman who is torn between being single and being married. In the heat of a disagreement, she will remind her husband who she is: "Don't you know who I am? I'm so and so! I don't need you! I don't need this!" She will have difficulty yielding to her husband because she will feel like she is still single even though she is married. Singleness is selfishness, and has no place in a marriage.

The Bottom line is a woman who hyphenates her name does not truly love her husband. When a woman is in love with a man, she desires his name and his children. Besides that, God called them **Adam**! Genesis 5:2 declares, *"Male and female created he them; and blessed them, and <u>called their name Adam</u>, in the day when they were created.*

I had some serious issues, and with a marriage teaching like that in the Church, while I was a baby saint, it didn't help me. All the while I was working on setting myself up career-wise, the Lord was telling me repeatedly that I was going to lose everything. After being saved for about two years, I was in the middle of making some financial decisions, and the Lord said to me, "One day, you will have nothing and will have to totally depend on me." I shook with fear on the inside when I heard Him say that. I was afraid to even think about it. Four years went by before it came to pass, and I lost everything. I thank the Lord; He gave me a good foundation in Him that had nothing to do with the material possessions He had given me.

"According to the grace of God which is given me, as a wise master builder, I have laid the foundation, and another buildeth thereon. But let every man take heed how he buildeth thereupon. For

other foundation can no man lay than that is laid, which is Jesus Christ. Now if any man build upon this foundation gold, silver, precious stones, wood, hay, stubble; Every man's work shall be made manifest: for the day shall declare it, because it shall be revealed by fire; and the fire shall try every man's work of what sort it is. If any man's work abide which he hath built thereupon, he shall receive a reward. If any man's work shall be burned, he shall suffer loss: but he himself shall be saved; yet so as by fire" (1st Corinthians 3:10-15).

In the natural, before my husband came for me, I had just purchased a home that was newly built from the ground up. I was living the things I only dreamed of before salvation. Life was good without a man and I still had mixed feelings about marriage. On the one hand, I desired companionship, and on the other, I desired independence. After three years of being saved, I tried to bargain with God and asked for a successful business instead of having a husband. That was when I realized I had completely lost sight of what God's plan was for me. The Lord told me at the beginning of my walk with Him that His plan was for me to have a husband because where He was taking me, I couldn't go alone.

Don't misunderstand me. I believe that women should be successful without a man. Don't put your dreams on hold, waiting for him to come. That's not what I am talking about. I'm talking about being so comfortable with enjoying the things you have accumulated that you refuse to receive your husband when he arrives and having a husband is the perfect will of God for YOUR life. I'm talking about those women whose accomplishments cloud their ability to discern the man of God they are supposed to marry when he shows up on the scene. The bottom line is no matter what things you accomplish they will fade away, but God can give you a Godly legacy that can't be measured by wealth.

Again, "*Lay not up for yourselves treasures upon earth, where moth and rust doth corrupt, and where thieves break through and steal: But lay up for yourselves treasures in heaven, where neither moth not rust doth corrupt, and where thieves do not break through and steal: For where your treasure is, there will your heart be also*" *(Matthew 6:19-21).* Desire the Lord's perfect and divine will for your life, especially if it includes a husband and a family because the Lord can use a Godly wife that has a Godly husband in many great ways.

Chapter 4

The <u>d</u>evil's Master Plan

"Be sober, be vigilant; because your adversary the devil, as a roaring lion, walketh about, seeking whom he may devour:"

1ˢᵗ Peter 5:8

CHAPTER 4: THE devil's MASTER PLAN

Instead of searching for a man, let the Lord build a strong Christian foundation under and in you. The devil would love for you to marry the wrong man because when you are not in God's divine will you will not be fully blessed. Don't except the permissive will of God. However, I caution you, usually, when the Lord permits something it will be with much tribulation. In the MWCD permissive means: granted on sufferance. Sufferance means patient endurance, longsuffering, pain, and misery. The Lord will allow you to move into His permissive will for your life, yet you will suffer, and you may lose some significant blessings you were supposed to enjoy and accomplish during that time frame. I caution you; it is better to accept the perfect will of God for your life. I have yet to see anyone who was blessed after they married someone they were not supposed to.

Romans 12:2 declares, *"And be not conformed to this world: but be ye transformed by the renewing of your mind, that ye may prove what is that good, and acceptable, and perfect, will of God."* The word perfect in the Merriam-Webster Collegiate Dictionary means being entirely without fault or defect: flawless, satisfying all requirements, and corresponding to an ideal standard.

47

There is something special about being in the Lord's perfect and divine will. If the promises of God are appointed for those in His perfect will, then where are the promises for those who settle for His permissive will? I strongly believe that there are no promises and few blessings. After all, Matthew 7:21 declares, *"Not every one that saith unto me, Lord, Lord, shall enter into the kingdom of heaven; but he that doeth the will of my Father which is in heaven."* Remember, only those that do the will of our Father in Heaven shall receive the Kingdom of Heaven, a promise that faithful Christians are waiting to inherit. This does not include those who do His permissive will.

The behavior of the world is to marry the person that YOU FEEL is the right person for you. That could be the person who looks good on the outside. The person who says all the things you would like for him to say. The person who does not go against what you believe. The person who fits right into your mold of life and who won't challenge you to change and be better is more than likely the person you will marry. You will marry the person that makes you comfortable. You may even be pressured to marry the person who pleases your family members and friends. When all along, the Lord desires to transform the way you think, even your way of life, so you can know and understand what His perfect will is for you.

After you know the Lord's will, He will begin to prove you. He will give you opportunities to make decisions the way you used to or to allow Him to guide you in your decisions. You will often be surprised because the Lord's guidance will be so contrary to what you are familiar with. And if you are a person that has many friends and family members who are your counselors, Godly or ungodly, then you will definitely be surprised to find that none will have a clue of what the Lord intends to do with you, because He will not tell them.

Many times, the Lord will have us to wait, and wait, and wait on His promises, making no move at all. This waiting is where we get into trouble. This is when the devil's plan goes into action to get the children of God out of the Lord's perfect will. The devil's plan is to keep our minds from being renewed. His plan is for us to keep desiring our own plan. The devil's plan is for us to not truly know what the Lord has for us. His plan is for us to not truly know whom the Lord has for us. The devil's plan is for us to be so caught up in getting a spouse that we are not working on crucifying our flesh and the lusts thereof. He desires us to be unprepared for ministry. His plan is for us to despise, fear, and dispute the will of God instead of readily accepting it.

"I delight to do thy will, O my God: yea, thy law is within my heart" Psalm 40:8. When we learn of the Lord's will for our lives and delight in doing it, we will see that the Lord will do all that He has promised. *"There failed not ought of any good thing which the Lord had spoken unto the house of Israel; all came to pass" (Joshua 21:45).*

There is not one person that I know who can say they have done absolutely everything the Lord has ever told them to do and the Lord still did not make good on His promises. If the Lord kept His promises concerning a rebellious nation of people, I know He will keep His promises to the obedient in Christ. The Lord will keep His promises even if He has to bless your bloodline to do it.

So, instead of accepting the Lord's permissive will, why not commit to doing only His divine and perfect will? Why not pray a prayer and ask the Lord to block you from anything in your life that is not in His divine will? This is what I did and still do. He sent my husband by His divine hand. Even though many people didn't like it, he was divinely sent from God and there was nothing any of us could do about it because I had sincerely asked God to govern my life.

After committing to wait on the Lord's perfect will, He began to work on my foundation with Him. He began to have me surrender more and more of myself. My understanding of His Word began to increase, and I began to do at home what I saw in the Church. I prayed for family members and friends and saw them healed of major physical issues that could only otherwise be healed through surgery. I saw supernatural financial blessings and debt cancellation. The Lord was manifesting His power in my life on the left and right.

I spent more and more time studying the Bible to understand how the Lord sees things. I took the time to teach my children about the Lord and prayed with them often. We were learning how to be Christians. It was an exciting time for me to come to know that the Lord God, our creator, is real.

The more I spent time with God, the more difficult situations in my life seemed like nothing. I fell more and more in love with the Lord. I know this sounds like a cliché, but it's not. I really worked on my personal relationship with Jesus. I didn't feel lonely nor did I crave the attention of a man. I felt like I could wait as long as the

Lord desired me to. It had gotten to the point where I was so content with the Lord that I loved being by myself, but for a different reason. This time it wasn't because I was afraid of a bad relationship, but it was because my relationship with Jesus felt so good.

The more time I spent with the Lord, He began to give me dreams about people in and out of the Church. I became His intercessor and prayer warrior. I became a soul winner for Him. I ministered to people on my job and on the streets. He came to trust me with information about other people. I was in prayer often for others, almost never for myself. I was thankful to be saved and truly desired to please God.

I began to ask Him for guidance concerning everything. I mean even the smallest thing in my life. I can remember times when I had to chastise my sons. I would first pray and ask the Lord to be in the midst of the situation and to give me wisdom on what to do. Sometimes He would say, "Spank them and sometimes He would say talk to them." There were times when I was fully set on spanking them, but the Lord would say, "No." My sons got a lot of comfort out of knowing that the Lord was concerned about them on this level. Still today, they go to their Heavenly Father and ask for what they call justice in various situations in their lives and He moves on their behalf.

I came to understand that the Lord is faithful. I came to love the Lord so much, that I began pouring my finances and time into the ministry I was attending. I was faithful in everything the Lord required of me. I offered freely of my talents and finances to move the Kingdom of God forward. I was sincere about my relationship with God. However, I was still naïve about a lot of things. The Lord allowed me to stay in that state of naivety so I could grow in the Word and build upon my relationship with Him.

I volunteered to work in children's Church and to sing in the choir. I worked faithfully on these auxiliaries for years. Then I worked with the evangelism team and the catechism department in different capacities, while still singing in the choir. I took as many Christian education classes, offered by the Church, as my schedule would allow. I even took classes on some Saturdays to learn as much as I could about the Lord. I did not let anything come between the Lord and me and what He was doing in my life.

Again, I read the Bible several times daily, making it a goal to read the Bible through. I took my Bible with me on business trips and often read on the airplane. I found websites where I could read the Bible on my available lunch breaks at work. I needed to know everything the Lord had promised me in His Word.

I became like the Jews of Berea, in the Book of Acts 17:10-11, searching the Scriptures daily to see if what they were teaching at Church was true. I made studying the Word a way of life. I remember someone telling me that single people were not complete unless they had a spouse. I immediately went to the Bible searching for Scriptures to see if that was true. I found that Jesus made me complete. My husband would not complete me, but I would compliment (praise and honor) and be a help meet for him. I would be my husband's glory. Additionally, my husband would be my head, spiritual covering, and tutor. Being single did not mean I was incomplete. Colossians 2:10, *"And ye are complete in him, which is the head of all principality and power:"*

I remember the Lord giving me specific instructions concerning what not to watch on television, what books to read or not read, and who to listen to on the radio. He began to govern my whole life. Then I decided not to watch television at all. I found a lot of time to spend with the Lord when I cut out the television. I didn't yearn for a social life like a lot of single Christians. I had no desire to go to Christian comedy or Christian clubs. I yearned to spend all my extra time with Jesus. I was so excited about being saved.

The Lord gave me the understanding of His Word to the point that I was able to discern the truth from error. I was also able to break the Word down and teach it to others. My spiritual gifts began to manifest more and more. The more time I spent with God, the more He anointed me. The Lord honored my fasting and anointed me for special fasts outside of what we did at the Church as a congregation. I was growing so rapidly that I didn't have time to think about dating. The Lord was laying a strong foundation under me.

Little did I know that this foundation that the Lord was building would be the very thing I'd have to stand on when my husband came for me; for the Church family and natural family whom I loved dearly didn't understand what the Lord was doing in my life, so they turned upon me to rend me ferociously like wolves.

"Whosoever cometh to me, and heareth my sayings, and doeth them, I will shew you to whom he is like: He is like a man which built an house, and digged deep, and laid the foundation on a rock: and when the flood arose, the stream beat vehemently upon that house,

and could not shake it: for it was founded upon a rock. But he that heareth, and doeth not, is like a man that without a foundation built an house upon the earth; against which the stream did beat vehemently, and immediately it fell; and the ruin of that house was great" (Luke 6:47-49).

Chapter 5

The Daughters of Zion

"In your patience possess ye your souls."

Luke 21:19

CHAPTER 5: THE DAUGHTERS OF ZION

"And it came to pass after this, that Absalom the son of David had a fair sister, whose name was Tamar; and Amnon the son of David loved her. And Amnon was so vexed, that he fell sick for his sister Tamar; for she was a virgin; and Amnon thought it hard for him to do any thing to her. But Amnon had a friend, whose name was Jonadab, the son of Shimeah David's brother: and Jonadab was a very subtle man" (2nd Samuel 13:1-3). [Subtle in the Merriam-Webster Collegiate Dictionary means delicate, elusive, perceptive, having keen eyesight].

"And he said unto him, Why art thou, being the king's son, lean from day to day? wilt thou not tell me? And Amnon said unto him, I love Tamar, my brother Absalom's sister. And Jonadab said unto him, Lay thee down on thy bed, and make thyself sick: and when thy father cometh to see thee, say unto him, I pray thee, let my sister Tamar come, and give me meat, and dress the meat in my sight, that I may see it, and eat it at her hand. So Amnon lay down, and made himself sick: and when the king was come to see him, Amnon said unto the king, I pray thee, let Tamar my sister come, and make me a couple of cakes in my sight, that I may eat at her hand. Then David sent home to Tamar, saying, Go now to thy brother Amnon's house,

and dress him meat. So Tamar went to her brother Amnon's house, and he was laid down. And she took flour, and kneaded it, and made cakes in his sight, and did bake the cakes" (2nd Samuel 13:5-8).

"And when she had brought them unto him to eat, he took hold of her, and said unto her, Come lie with me, my sister. And she answered him, Nay, my brother, do not force me; for no such thing ought to be done in Israel: do not thou this folly. And I, whither shall I cause my shame to go? And as for thee, thou shalt be as one of the fools in Israel. Now, therefore, I pray thee, speak unto the king; for he will not withhold me from thee. Howbeit he would not hearken unto her voice: but, being stronger than she, forced her, and lay with her. Then Amnon hated her exceedingly; so that the hatred wherewith he hated her was greater than the love wherewith he had loved her. And Amnon said unto her, Arise, be gone" (2nd Samuel 13:11-15).

Many sisters in the Church slip, tip, and midnight dip with men who pretend to be their brothers in Christ. The truth is many of these brothers only have a plan to satisfy their flesh. When sisters in the Church undermine leadership and date without permission, they open themselves up to being pressured or forced into sexual intercourse. To add to her shame, the one she dates ends up hating her more than the lust he had for her; and she is left with no hope of being married.

The only thing that comes from a situation like this is emotional and social damage, a nullified testimony, shame and reproach on the Gospel, and possibly reproach on the ministry she is attending. Sisters in Christ need to realize that just because a brother says that he is saved, it doesn't mean he has crucified his flesh and the lusts thereof. Galatians 5:24 declares, *"And they that are Christ's have crucified the flesh with the affections and lusts."*

The Best thing for a sister to do to avoid this situation is to learn how to possess her own vessel in holiness and not to put anything past her flesh. Dating should only be with the man you are preparing to marry. It should not be to pass time or experiment. Don't tell yourself you can handle it. And make sure you don't tell yourself, "I can always ask for forgiveness if I fall." Because although you may ask for and receive forgiveness, it doesn't mean you will not have to pay for your sin in some form or fashion later.

Many Christians think it is okay to operate in foreplay as long as they are not having intercourse, but the truth is any form of foreplay is sin. Besides, you never know what you are dealing with when it comes to flesh or a man. Most of the time, men do not like foreplay alone and some could have a track record of forcing themselves on women. Again, just because someone is saved, it doesn't mean they have overcome this area of their life; and even if they have abstained from sex, it doesn't mean they are not human. And if they have crucified the flesh, tempting it will be like waking up a sleeping giant.

The bottom line is foreplay and intercourse outside of the marriage covenant are both sins. Therefore, ladies, I admonish you, *"In your patience possess ye your souls" (Luke 21:19).* Patience in Strong's Concordance means cheerful endurance, patient waiting, and constancy. In addition, possess means to get, acquire, own, obtain, possess, provide, and purchase – your own soul.

About four years into my salvation, at the direction of our Church overseer, several hundred single women in the ministry met for one hour after each weekly Bible study. We were called, "Daughters of Zion." Initially, we were supposed to meet for a month or two. However, the meetings continued for eight months. We came together to pray for the Lord to send our husbands. Although there were many married couples in the ministry, there were still more women that were single, and not enough single brothers to go around. And the single brothers were afraid to get married.

"Daughters of Zion" represented women of virtue, holiness, obedience, and faithfulness. We promised to conform to the will of God and abstain from fornication. We promised to allow the Lord to set us aside and apart for the man He had for us. No longer would we be subjected to the dating game. We promised to keep ourselves pure so we could be presentable by God at the time we were to be united in holy matrimony.

We also promised to walk in every aspect of His Word and remain in faithfulness, trusting God, and waiting for Him to send our Godly husbands. We promised to no longer approach men. We were told to purchase a ring to put on a finger of our right hand as a reminder of the vows we took. We were not to remove the ring until our husbands came to take it off.

It was while we were having these meetings that the truth was manifested about the man I thought was my husband, as described in Chapter 2. It was in these prayer sessions that I had to break through the walls of fear of being married. It was also in these meetings that I let go of some personal insecurities concerning men and marriage. I grew to love my sisters in the Body of Christ more because we had come together in prayer to pray for a common goal.

At this time, I began to pray for my true husband whom I did not know. Later, I found out that during the time that we had these meetings my husband was living in a foreign country. He was facing a serious trial in his life and my prayers for him were being answered even though he was 4,000 miles away.

I prayed for his strength, his relationship with the Lord, his obedience to Christ, and that the Lord would make me the wife that he needed. I desired to be the woman of God that would stand by him when no one else would. I knew that he would be a man of great authority in the spirit realm and I needed to be in a certain place in the Lord to be ready for him.

In one of the meetings, we received deliverance from a spirit that had been operating in my natural family for generations, the spirit of Jezebel. Now, that I am in ministry with my husband, I understand more about what Jezebel's spirit, as in the Bible, really was. Jezebel hated God and all that He represented. She hated the people of God and would do whatever possible to destroy those who carried the Word of the Lord.

The woman who is like Jezebel hates Godly men and will do whatever she can to bring the man of God down to take his place. She has a strong spiritual relationship with those in the heavenlies, but the relationship is not with the Lord. Sometimes women are told they have a Jezebel spirit because they are controlling or use the way they look to manipulate men, yet these were not the only things Jezebel operated in. Jezebel knew what she was doing for she operated in witchcrafts. She was a rebellious and cursed woman. *"Go, see now this cursed woman, and bury her: for she is a king's daughter" (2ⁿᵈ Kings 9:34d-g). "What peace, so long as the whoredoms of thy mother Jezebel and her witchcrafts are so many" (2ⁿᵈ Kings 9:22g-h).*

Jezebel despised and hated the prophets of the Lord. *"And Ahab called Obadiah, which was the governor of his house. (Now Obadiah feared the Lord greatly: For it was so, when <u>Jezebel cut off the prophets of the Lord</u>, that Obadiah took an hundred prophets, and hid them by fifty in a cave, and fed them with bread and water)" (1ˢᵗ Kings 18:3-4).*

Jezebel was always in competition with her husband. Instead of him leading her, she was instructing and directing him to do evil. *"But Jezebel his wife came to him, and said unto him, why is thy*

65

spirit so sad, that thou eatest no bread? And he said unto her,
Because I spake unto Naboth the Jezreelite, and said unto him, Give
me thy vineyard for money; or else, if it please thee, I will give thee
another vineyard for it: and he answered, I will not give thee my
vineyard. And Jezebel his wife said unto him, Dost thou now govern
the kingdom of Israel? arise, and eat bread, and let thine heart be
merry: I will give thee the vineyard of Naboth the Jezreelite," (1st
Kings 21:5-7). Jezebel was able to operate the way she did because
she was stronger than her husband. Her counselors were false
prophets. She knew who her god was and it was not the Lord
Jehovah. She was a worshipper of Baal, according to 1st Kings 16:31.

One way we know that the enemy is strategically planning to
destroy a marriage union, institution, organization, or country, etc. is
we will see the woman begin to reposition herself. The enemy will
begin to attack the woman who will then entice her husband to sin.
Eve is a prime example, Genesis 3:4-6 declares, *"And the serpent*
said unto the woman, Ye shall not surely die: For God doth know that
in the day ye eat thereof, then your eyes shall be opened, and ye shall
be as gods, knowing good and evil. And when the woman saw that the
tree was good for food, and that it was pleasant to the eyes, and a tree

66

to be desired to make one wise, she took of the fruit thereof, and did eat, and gave also unto her husband with her; and he did eat."

Likewise, today, a woman who is operating in the same spirit as Jezebel will have like characteristics. She is the woman who will call herself Bishop, Apostle, or Prophet so and so. She will do things that are CONTRARY to the Word of God and say, "God gave me a revelation." Whatever God is in, it will line up with the Word of God. I don't believe the Lord is even speaking to the woman who disrespects her husband, doesn't submit to headship, or has placed herself in a position of authority above her husband's position. If a woman is doing this, she is in rebellion, PERIOD! This is the true Jezebel spirit.

Think about it, a Bishop is a HUSBAND of one wife according to 1st Timothy 3:2b. An Apostle, according to Strong's Concordance, is defined as one sent, HE who is sent. Even in Scripture, Jesus gave us examples of how God has set up authority in His Body. He didn't choose any women Apostles. A Prophet is a MAN and we know a man can be in a position of headship. A woman, who is called a Prophetess, can never be the head. She must have her head covered by her husband.

Even the Scripture declares that a woman who has the inspired gift of utterance is called a Prophetess, not a Prophet. In Luke 2:36 Anna was called a Prophetess, not a Prophet. There is no woman Prophetess in the Bible that was called a Prophet, period! A woman with the Jezebel spirit will change the Word of God to fit her desires. A woman with a Jezebel spirit will not be comfortable being a woman, so she will always be trying to make herself equal to or put herself above the man.

When a woman places herself in a position of headship, by calling herself any title reserved for males, things change in the spirit realm and she opens doors to be attacked by the enemy, even to be attacked by her husband, because the man will feel the power struggle in the spirit realm. It is in man's nature to defend his place of authority, even if it's unconsciously.

A woman that is in a power struggle with her husband will cause friction in the home and may not realize that her repositioning herself is the source. A woman who is operating in this spirit will never be able to dwell with a truly Godly man in peace. She will never yield to true authority and she will hate to see the children of God prosper.

Now that I've gone through deliverance in this area, I now understand that with my family background, it was important for me to attend this deliverance session. Because I would be a prime candidate for the enemy to deceive me to become like Jezebel. After I married, I came to understand that the "Daughters of Zion" deliverance session did not reveal all the doors where this Jezebel spirit could follow me around and try to operate in my life. Since the Lord called me to minister beside my husband, who is an Apostle, I had to go through some more serious deliverance, at which time the matriarch spirit was identified. It operates alongside the Jezebel spirit. Both mindsets had to go completely in order for me to effectively operate in ministry.

Chapter 6

He Found Me. How Did it Happen?

"Who can find a virtuous woman? for her price is far above rubies."

Proverbs 31:10

CHAPTER 6: HE FOUND ME. HOW DID IT HAPPEN?

At the end of 2000, on the cusp of the new year, the Lord told me, and I shared it with a Christian friend at the Church, that we both would meet our husbands in the next year. In the fall of 2001, there was an evangelism meeting at the Church on a Friday evening. I was one of the evangelism secretaries and usually sat on the front row. On this particular day, I was late arriving to the meeting, which never happened before, causing me to have to sit several rows from the front. Since I came in late, we ended up sitting next to each other. Then I heard the words in my spirit, "This man shall be your husband." Immediately I thought, "The devil is a liar. I'm not getting caught up in this again." I was thinking about being tricked again like I mentioned in Chapter two; so, I kept it to myself.

Some months went by and I noticed that he was showing interest in me, but I had mixed feelings about what was happening. I didn't know how to handle the situation since it was now over five years into my salvation walk and I was extremely nervous about what was getting ready to happen. I hadn't had the attention of a man in nearly six years and wasn't sure what to expect.

I didn't have any dreams and the only thing the Lord said to me about him at the time was to not say anything bad about him. I'm glad the Lord told me this because people started talking about him to me, so I was already prepared to hold my peace.

By this time, we were both working on the evangelism team, making little or no contact with each other, and yet his interest in me grew. The more I felt that he was interested, the more I ran the other way. Sometimes I would even feel that he desired for me to look in his direction so he could wave hello, but I made a point to not give him any attention. I found out later, that the Lord was drawing him to me although he was not particularly interested in being involved with anyone. He was especially not interested in getting married.

At the beginning of the year, the ministry added another choir, which meant the choir I was in sang every other week. One day when we were scheduled to sing, he said he was sitting in the sanctuary and saw a beam of light over me. The beam of light looked like something out of the original Star Trek television show. He looked around and asked someone else if they saw what he saw. After he was told no, then he knew that what he saw was only for him.

After two weeks went by, we were scheduled to sing again and he saw another beam of light. We had about 60 people in the choir at the time and there is a beam of light over me for a second time. He said he knew he was supposed to talk to me. Immediately following service, he approached me to let me know that he saw beams of light over me and the second beam had the words holy, holy, holy unto the Lord in it. I knew he was not lying because only the Lord and I knew that I was walking upright and correct and not playing games with my salvation. Even though he told me what he saw, I still did not fully understand its significance.

After this, I began to be more and more interested in him, but he was not rushing anything. Then one day he invited me to go skating with the youth ministry that was planning a skating party. I was shocked and told him, "No!" I thought within myself, "Skating! I haven't skated in years and wasn't too good at it then!" My attitude was terrible, especially since I later found out that he had already purchased the tickets. One day during an evangelism meeting, we were getting ready for a Saturday outing. Since it was raining, the Pastor over the group said we should eat some pizza and go to some nearby businesses and walk around looking for opportunities to minister to some individuals. It was a scarce turn out of volunteers so we ended up in teams of two and with individuals whom we would not normally work with.

As I was getting some pizza, I set my purse in a chair next to where I knew he'd be sitting and a Deacon in the Church moved my purse to another chair. When I went back to the table, I realized my purse and chair were moved and the Deacon was smiling. I was stunned and couldn't understand why he would move my purse. I tried to move my chair next to him again, but the more I did, the more the Deacon seemed upset and was trying to block the two of us from talking.

When it was time to go out and evangelize, I selected my future husband as a partner and the day went well. We flowed together by the Holy Spirit and were able to pray for some people in a nearby department store. Afterward, he walked me to my car and we didn't speak again personally for some time.

Then one day he started asking me questions. I thought this was strange because he was asking me things like, "Are you controlling?" I was thinking, what! No! Yes! I don't know! On another day he said, "Are you obedient?" I didn't answer. I chose to ask someone else in the Church and she said, "Yes, you are too obedient to leadership." Then on yet another day, he said, "Are you married?" I said, "No!" I was livid! I wondered, what's with all the questions? After that, he didn't ask me any more questions.

Then surprisingly, as I was leaving the sanctuary one day, running in my spirit from him as fast as I could, as I'd done on many occasions, he was outside the sanctuary standing by the wall near the door and he says, "Why are you running?" Another sister in the Church who was with me said, "Is he bothering you? I have your back." We all laughed. I was so afraid of what the Lord was about to do, I was running from my blessing. However, my frustration was about to hit the fan. On another day, he had a conversation with me and asked, "Do you have a business?" I said, "Yes!" I thought, "This is it, he's finally going to ask me out." But he didn't! He started saying maybe I can help you with your business. I thought, "What!" Then I said, "Look, I don't know what your intentions are, but I don't give my number out to guys and I don't need help with my business." Then I walked away. Suddenly I walked back over to him and said, "Listen, don't step to me like that, when you step to me you better step to me right, and know what you want!" He had the biggest smile on his face. I was boiling! While walking the parking lot to go to my car, I said, "Lord, please tell him to leave me alone!"

In March, we were both participating in a Resurrection Sunday play that was being presented by the ministry. I had to go to Canada for a week on a business trip with my boss and knew that even though he and I were not dating yet, he would miss my presence during the rehearsals. The Lord was setting the stage for our courtship.

It was a Wednesday after I returned from Canada. The rehearsals were still going on and he came up to me during the last week of rehearsals and invited me out again. He said, "Maybe there was some misunderstanding the last time I asked you to go skating. What I was trying to say was I'd like to take you out." I said, "Can you repeat that, I'm not sure what you said," and he said, "I'd like to ask you out." Then suddenly it was time to rehearse, and we bowed our heads to open up in prayer. Immediately after rehearsal, I left and went home without answering him.

On Thursday, I had made up my mind that I wasn't going to give him an answer because, at this point, I felt he was playing games. I thought within myself, "I'll give him an answer by the summer, and if he's still interested in taking me out at that time, then I'll know he's serious." I spoke with a married woman that I knew through work who was a Christian. The Lord told her to tell me to speak with him, give him an answer, and do not ignore him. And definitely don't make him wait until the summer.

Then it happened. I had a dream early Friday morning. The dream was clear. We were both in the Church at rehearsal for the play. And everyone in the Church was angry because we were dating. They were spreading lies about him, and he held his peace. I stood up and began to defend him. The people in the dream were from the choir, the youth department, and those who typically participated in theatrical events at the Church. The leader of the drama department was only an observer in the dream and wasn't saying anything. When I awoke from this dream, I knew I was going to date him. Because I felt that if everyone was against it, the Lord must be in it. I know my thinking is not traditional; it has never been all my life.

That Friday night, we were preparing to perform in the play. When he saw me, he immediately approached me and said, "The Lord told me to ask you about the dream you had." I was surprised that he knew. I just looked at him and didn't say anything. He continued to press the issue by saying, "I know you had a dream because the Lord told me that you did." I was stunned because no one had ever told me the Lord told them anything about a dream I had. This conversation was just the beginning stages of my understanding of how much the Lord talked with him about many things. I didn't share the dream with him that day because I didn't desire it to influence any decisions he would have to make.

He let the issue go, and we continued to talk briefly before stepping into another area to iron our costumes. That's when he said to me, "You are playing hard to get. You didn't give me an answer," about a date. I said to him, "I'm going to give you an answer, don't rush me." I finished ironing and went to get dressed. As I dressed for the play, he sat at the table and joked with my two sons as they ate take-out dinner.

Later, everyone assembled backstage to prepare to start the production. As we waited, we made eye contact and couldn't stop looking at each other. The sparks were flying between us, no words were spoken, yet the cast saw the sparkle in both our eyes. Several saints were smiling, making comments, and showing surprise about what they saw happening with us.

When the play was over, we talked about going out again, yet, this time, he was talking about taking my children with us. I said, "No! If we go, we go. I don't believe children should be subjected to the dating process at this point." I thought like this because the children would not be emotionally involved if things didn't work out. Then the Bishop of the Church walked over to our table and shook his hand. That was the night I asked the Bishop for permission to date him. He said, "Yes, he seems to have a good heart." And I was to keep him informed of what was going on.

I have to say, I never told the Bishop anything because I remembered the Bishop's wife saying she doesn't tell anyone anything and she didn't tell anyone anything when they were dating. And I fully believe that if a woman desires to marry someone, she has to be careful not to talk about that person to anyone because he could lose trust for her, as the Bishop once instructed us in a marriage teaching. The two will need to learn how to have a relationship together that doesn't include a whole lot of other people. So, with the Bishop's permission, I gave him my phone number.

Chapter 7

My Big Question

*"But seek ye first the Kingdom of God, and his
righteousness; and all these things shall be added unto
you."*

Matthew 6:33

CHAPTER 7: MY BIG QUESTION

"Therefore I say unto you, Take no thought for your life, what ye shall eat, or what ye shall drink; nor yet for your body, what ye shall put on. Is not the life more than meat, and the body than raiment? Behold the fowls of the air: for they sow not, neither do they reap, nor gather into barns; yet your heavenly Father feedeth them. Are ye not much better than they? Which of you by taking thought can add one cubit unto his stature? And why take ye thought for raiment? Consider the lilies of the field, how they grow; they toil not, neither do they spin: And yet I say unto you, That even Solomon in all his glory was not arrayed like one of these. Wherefore, if God so clothe the grass of the field, which to day is, and to morrow is cast into the oven, shall he not much more clothe you, O ye of little faith? Therefore take no thought, saying, What shall we eat? or, What shall we drink? or, Wherewithal shall we be clothed? (For after all these things do the Gentiles seek:) for your heavenly Father knoweth that ye have need of all these things. But seek ye first the Kingdom of God, and his righteousness; and all these things shall be added unto you. Take therefore no thought for the morrow: for the morrow shall take

thought for the things of itself. Sufficient unto the day is the evil thereof" (Matthew 6:25-34).

I spent a lot of time at the beginning of my walk with the Lord cleaning up my debt and continuing to build my financial portfolio. I desired to make sure I could bring material wealth to the table when I met my husband. When I started dating my future husband, the first major question I asked him was, how will you take care of my sons and me? I have a house with responsibilities. How can you take care of me? His response was something like, "I will trust the Lord to provide what we need at the proper time if we are to be married." This was so funny because we were only talking on the phone for a week, and I was already considering this man's pockets.

Primarily, this concern was not really from me, but it was a manifestation of all the seeds that had been planted by other people I knew, both at work and in the Church. Other people saw me a certain way and assumed that the Lord would send me a husband of great material substance. Other people had this expectation of what my husband would be, but I knew deep down inside that we would have small beginnings. Before we met, I remember my Pastor's sister once spoke in front of the Church. She was talking about the Pastor's wife when they first got engaged and how she had a diamond in her engagement ring that was so small that she needed a magnifying glass to see it. However, she was so in love at the time of their engagement that she didn't see the diamond as small. She was so appreciative of what the Lord was doing in her life that she was not concerned about the small beginnings.

While speaking, she turned to the congregation and said, "I hear the Lord saying for someone here, do not despise small beginnings." I was immediately quickened in my spirit and knew the Lord was talking to me because I had this thing about being given a large carat diamond ring. I often wondered how this small beginning would come to be. I now think about how the Lord told me that one day I wasn't going to have any money and would have to totally depend on him. These two things were tied together, and I didn't know it.

I also remember when my sons and I were on a business trip in Chicago. While we were traveling, the Lord spoke to me and said, "I'm going to bless your socks off." I was so excited about the word of the Lord. Then when we came back home and went to Church, the Bishop said, "There is a sister here. The Lord told me to tell you that he is sending you a husband that is going to bless your socks off!" My spirit leaped. I was so excited because I knew the Lord was confirming what he had already said, and to top it off, the Lord was saying that this blessing was going to come through my husband.

So, even though people were telling me what I needed in a man, the Lord was telling me something totally different. When my husband came for me, we didn't have a problem with what the Lord's plan was for our lives; it was other people who had a problem with what the Lord was going to put us through. 1st Peter 5:10 declares, *"But the God of all grace, who hath called us unto his eternal glory by Christ Jesus, after that ye have suffered a while, make you perfect, stablish, strengthen, settle you."* I was convinced that these people didn't desire to suffer or give up anything for the Lord, so they didn't desire for me to grow through sufferance either. They were only seeking prosperity. 2nd Timothy 2:11 and 2:12 a-b declares, *"It is a faithful saying: For if we be dead with him, we shall also live with him: If we suffer, we shall also reign with him:"*

The truth is, in order to grow, we have to first die to self, and sometimes we have to give some things up, and other times we have to give up everything. Mark 10:29-30 declares, *"And Jesus answered and said, Verily I say unto you, There is no man that hath left house, or brethren, or sisters, or father, or mother, or wife, or children, or lands, for my sake, and the gospel's, But he shall receive a hundredfold now in this time, houses, and brethren, and sisters, and mothers, and children, and lands, with persecutions; and in the world to come eternal life."*

After my conversation with my future spouse that day about how he would care for us, I continued to pray. I was disturbed because I felt this man did not have enough substance to care for me. Basically, I tried to keep a certain lifestyle. The situation was: the Lord was sending him back to America after spending his adult life in another country. Even though his lifestyle was greater than what I'd experienced here in America, he had to get re-established. This man owned Audi's and Porsche's and vacationed in some of the finest places in the world. Something I had never experienced. The Lord had stripped him of everything, and it would take time for him to rebuild in America.

So, a few days after this conversation, one of my catechism students said, "I was praying for you, and the Lord gave me a word for you." I went and got an Elder to judge the word, and this is what the Lord said, "The man I am sending you will lack nothing, he will have everything he needs, but you have to be patient." The Elder asked if I understood the word. I said, "No." He replied, "This is an answer to your prayers." You're concerned about this, and the Lord said, "Don't be concerned because he will lack nothing." That was enough for me. I never spoke about him caring for me or my sons, or a lack of finances since. And we have lacked nothing! The Lord has been providing our needs supernaturally.

Also, what I didn't know was that he would be accused of being with me because of what people thought I had materially. The truth was I was not making as much money as many thought, but because it was more than a lot of people in my circle they thought it was a lot. Also, I was giving much of that which I had to the Church and not to him as many had accused me of. Then the Lord told me to quit my job so he could take me on the journey of my life. This would be a journey where I had to totally depend upon the Lord, as he told me four years earlier.

Before I actually quit my job, a 15-year career, I went to the Church and spoke with an Elder to get counsel on what I should do. He told me that he couldn't tell me what to do; I had to be sure myself what the Lord was telling me to do. He also told me to make sure that I was financially ready. Then he went to two ministers and asked them to prophesy to me. These were prophecies, all of which have come to pass, confirming what the Lord was about to do in my life. One thing that was said in particular was, "You are going to start to see things differently." This certainly happened. After I quit my job, I was reminded of another word someone gave me earlier in the year indicating the Lord was going to release me from my job.

So, what's the point of this chapter? Don't have a predefined list of what your spouse is going to be like, because if he doesn't fit the script, you may miss your blessing.

Chapter 8

Don't Be Mad at Me and My Blessing

"Be not deceived; God is not mocked: for whatsoever a man soweth, that shall he also reap."

Galatians 6:7

CHAPTER 8: DON'T BE MAD AT ME AND MY BLESSING

In the spring, we went out on our first date. It was an interesting day because on our first date we went to a park and walked and talked for hours. He was very cautious and I was extremely excited. This dating process would soon prove to be a wakeup call for me because I thought everyone would be happy for me, but they weren't.

Once we started dating, I found out that a lot of women in the Church liked him and some men in the Church liked me. It was the strangest thing because many of the women with whom I was acquainted thought he was to be their husband and that caused their relationship with me to change. Also, I couldn't understand what the problem was with the men. We were in the Church for years and they showed no interest in me until my husband came.

I was so immature when it came to Church-folk that I was hurt and extremely disappointed by how people carried themselves while we were dating. I found out that Church-folk are still human with real human emotions and issues. One of the most memorable situations was with a woman who was a leader in the Church. My future spouse joined an auxiliary she was over and, somehow, she thought he was to be her husband. She openly expressed her interest in him to several people and in several meetings.

Then one day following Sunday Church service, after we had been dating for several weeks, she actually grabbed him, sat him down, and started to tell him how he should have let her know he was dating me. She was so angry that she got in his face, pointed her finger at him, and proceeded to rail on him; mainly questioning him about why he was with me. Afterwards, he told her the Bishop had given us permission to date. She was shocked and said, "It's not going to last."

The whole time we were dating she refused to hug me when the Bishop said, "Hug your neighbor." If I greeted her, she would walk away from me without speaking and would roll her eyes when she saw me. This went on for months. To make peace, I went as far as to purchase a card for her. I placed a love offering in it to encourage her that the Lord was going to bless her for her faithfulness. That didn't work and she actually got worse; boy was I foolish. It was crazy! She was at least 40 years old, but when this man came to the ministry, she acted like a teenager in high school. What made it even more shameful was that she was assigned to teach other single

Christians how to walk before the Lord and prepare themselves for their spouses.

Then there was another spiritual leader on one of the same auxiliaries that I was on who also liked him. She was in her early forties and had been married several times already. When she found out we were dating, she gave me looks like I wasn't good enough for him. She also stopped speaking to me and was not as warm toward me as she had been in the previous five years. She was also acting like a child. I have seen more Christian women convert back to carnality when a new man came to the Church than I ever care to experience in life again.

There was another sister who actually told him to ask her out on a date so they could fall in love, get married, and have children. He told her that he was not the man to be her husband. In truth, he told her that her husband was not at that Church. She received him with disappointment but still changed toward me because she was friends with one of the women who also thought he was her husband. Two friends thinking, hoping, the same man is to be their husband. What a mess! I couldn't believe it! I thought I was closer to this particular sister because we served in the ministry together for many years.

After a while, she came to her senses, repented to me, and started treating me as she had before, as a sister in Christ. She was not a leader in the Church, but she was more mature than some of the female leaders I encountered in this situation.

Then there was the sister in the Church, who never had a problem dating anyone in the Church. She always had men chasing after her and asking her for dates and to marry them. She had a couple of marriage proposals where they actually purchased a ring, but nothing came of it. It seemed as if she had already dated every available man in the Church and had plenty more as backups. However, when my divine connection came, even though she was not interested in him, she had a problem that I would probably be getting married. She could not stand the idea that the Lord would bless me with a husband. She desired to get married before me to prove that she was something more than I was. What she didn't know was, I was hoping and praying that the Lord would give her a husband and allow her to marry before I did. This sister's desire to be married spilled over into jealousy and anger. In fact, she was so angry that she started to spread a lot of vicious lies and rumors about me. Unfortunately, a lot of people believed her, including the spiritual leaders of the Church.

Then there was the sister who clearly didn't like me, and desired to be all in my business. So, she constantly asked me, "When are you getting married?" Every time I turned around, she was asking me this question, and yet she never had any nice words to say to me before I started dating. I knew she did not really care whether I was getting married or not, she was just being nosy. So, finally, I answered her and said, "Can a sister just have a date?" She stopped asking after that. I know she thought I was being mean, but I felt like we had been in that Church all those years and the only previous conversation she had with me was one where she desired to tear my head off, so why is she in my face now?

Then there was a Christian sister whom I thought was mature enough to be truly happy for me. We talked about my new blessing because she saw that I was so happy. She was always asking me if we were still dating and what was going on. She was very specific about her questions: did he take you out, have you kissed yet, etc? She would say, "Oh, I'm so excited for you." Then one day the Lord told me not to tell her anything else because she was jealous. I thought,

"What!" So, the next time I talked with her on the phone, she said she had to confess something to me and hoped I would not take it the wrong way. She actually said, when you told me about your blessing, I became jealous. I was shocked! I didn't hold this against her because she was being honest. Once I married my divine connection, I became very careful about what I said to her concerning my marriage. Unfortunately, we could not remain friends because of her jealousy.

It's amazing to me that people do things not realizing that we are spiritual beings and many of us have spiritual gifts and can discern what they are thinking. In some cases, I could see the true nature of their spirits concerning my divine connection, and I never said anything. I grew up quickly in this area and came to understand that no one that I knew, who was single, was happy for me.

Then there were brothers in the Church, some were leaders, who couldn't believe I was dating. They were actually jealous because another man was appointed to marry me. What really got me was when married men started making comments. One of them said to my future husband, "Man, you are blessed. She is one of the finest women in this Church." I felt so uncomfortable when I heard him say it because I knew his wife.

Another one, who was a married leader, felt I shouldn't have been dating my future husband because of his haircut. He said to my eleven-year-old son, "Your momma likes him with that haircut?" How shallow! If I married him for a haircut I'd be in trouble. This is the same married man that was telling single sisters in the Church that his wife forced him to marry her. So, he thinks his lust for single women is okay as long as they stay single.

This is one of the married leaders who were telling single sisters in the Church what rating they were amongst the other women on a scale from one to ten. What a bunch of mess! This same leader told me one day, "My wife said: quiet as it is kept you are very pretty." He tried to make me believe his wife was saying this about me, not knowing that I know women do not talk that way about other women, especially not to their husbands.

Then there were all the people who were approaching my two sons and planting negative seeds about my potential spouse. They had messed up my sons so much with their negativity that the initial trust they had in the Lord diminished. Even the excitement my youngest son had concerning my future husband was overshadowed by negative things that were being spoken in his ears when we went to Church.

Initially, when my son met him at eleven, he told me, "Mom it's okay to marry him. He's good people." We were always taught that children will know the truth about a person, so I pondered on what he said. After all the negativity, my sons began to have doubts and spiritual battles concerning our future marriage. I had failed to guard them.

Now, I can say they have learned the truth for themselves. I would also like to say that when my eldest son was separated from the Lord, no one cared that he was on his way to hell, but when he renewed his relationship with the Lord and began to strive toward the Lord and walk in holiness under the leadership of my husband, he started getting correspondence from the same immature married leader in the Church saying he had a dream about him in hell. I knew that he was only saying this because he felt he should not be associating with me and my husband.

My eldest son told me that he noticed when he was in sin, no one from the Church said anything to him. They actually embraced him and constantly told him he was okay when he was the furthest away from God. When he came back home with my husband and me and was encouraged to get his relationship right with the Lord, now the same leader claimed he was going to hell.

If you have young children, guard them because the enemy will use family members, friends, Church members, and Church leaders to speak into their ears to come out against what the Lord is doing in your life. All I can say to people who hate on other people when the Lord blesses them is lookout because you will reap what you sow! Galatians 6:7, *"Be not deceived; God is not mocked: for whatsoever a man soweth, that shall he also reap."* No matter how much time goes by; even if you forget what you've done, there is a record in Heaven and you will reap at an inopportune time.

The word "whatsoever" in Galatians 6:7 doesn't have a definition in Strong's Concordance or Vines Dictionary, implying that there is no limit to the type of seeds that a person can sow. Things that we count as a small thing will come back on us in a greater measure. And remember exactly what you sow is what you will reap. You will not reap apples if you sowed seeds for oranges. "Reap" in

Strong's Concordance means: in the sense of the crop, harvest, or reap.

In the Merriam-Webster Collegiate Dictionary, crop is the yield of a field; harvest is the <u>season for gathering</u> in agricultural crops, the act or process of <u>gathering an accumulated store</u> or productive result. As you continue to mistreat people, you will one day reach the season for gathering your accumulated store. All the evil you dished out will come back on YOU when you least expect it!

Some people think just because they have gone through some hardship, they are reaping what they sowed. No! The actual mess you sowed is what you are going to get back. If you tried to destroy someone's relationship, then one day someone is going to try to destroy your relationship. And it will be the relationship that you desperately desire to work. All of the gossip and lies that you spread are going to come upon you. All of the discord you sowed in the house of God is going to one day return unto you. The same pain you caused someone else is going to be magnified to you again! *"for it must needs be that offenses come; but woe to that man by whom the offence cometh" (Matthew 18:7b-c)!*

Chapter 9

My Sister, My Daughter, My Mother, My Friend, My Rival

"For who maketh thee to differ from another? and what hast thou that thou didst not receive? now if thou didst receive it, why dost thou glory, as if thou hadst not received it."

1st Corinthians 4:7

CHAPTER 9: MY SISTER, MY DAUGHTER, MY MOTHER, MY FRIEND, MY RIVAL

Have you ever wondered why many women don't get along and basically have little or no trust toward each other? Are you a woman that feels uncomfortable around other women? Did you ever walk into a room or down a street and women turned and stared at you until you were seated or out of sight? Have you ever had other women dislike you without a reason? I know you've heard this statement made by women, "I don't like her, she thinks she's all that," or you may have heard, "she thinks she looks good in that outfit." Instead of compliments, she is criticized. Have you ever wondered why? Selah.

Have you ever known a woman that thought she was better than you because of the color of her skin or eyes, the size or shape of her body, the length of her hair, or her social and economic status? Have you ever believed it? Have you had someone dislike you for any of these reasons or again, no reason at all? Have you ever wondered why? Selah.

Do you know any women that don't respect other women's relationships? Have you ever been around a woman that thought she was the most beautiful woman in a group of women? She's the type of woman that will go as far as telling you she looks better than you do and that all men want her. You may have heard other women plotting to take someone else's man or only become interested in a certain man when they see a certain woman with him. Has someone close to you ever flirted or slept with your man behind your back or in your face? How did you handle it?

Have you ever supposedly lost a man to another woman? When you found out you were sharing a man, what did you do? Even though we know the pain of rejection and deceit this causes our sisters, have you ever wondered why women continue to hurt other women? Why do we continue the cycle?

Women do some of the strangest things. I know you've noticed that women often compete with each other for a man's attention. I have seen women endure unkind mistreatment by men to keep from losing them to another woman. Lose him! The famous words, "I don't want to lose you!" Is it a game, contest, war, or other competitive sport? The way women behave one would think so.

Women have been exploited since the early ages of time, and have given their minds, bodies, and dreams to please a man. I've even seen my sisters in the Body of Christ despise, ensnare, scheme, lie, and even hate for a mate. A woman that does this doesn't know who she is and hasn't truly tapped into the power of God. My sisters, God is saying it doesn't have to be so.

When the Lord sends the man of God He has for you, you won't have to reduce yourselves to worldly ways to keep him or to cause him to love you. What the Lord Jesus has for you is for you. The power of God is able to send that man who will truly love and respect you as God's daughter. This means you don't have to feel pressured into sexual relations before marriage. Frankly, sexual intercourse is marriage, even according to Scripture. Therefore, in essence, the marriage license is permission to have intercourse or it deems intercourse lawful. It is man's way of determining who has rights to a spouse's estate.

Oftentimes the women are orchestrating this type of affection with a man because this is what women do to get his attention. Women change their outer appearance to get that physical attraction going. This is how they compete with other women. I truly believe this is why God has so many single women in the Body of Christ. Many are not ready for the true man of God.

Think about this. God has many Godly men with a great work ahead of them. The Lord desires to reveal His daughters to the men and unite them in Holy matrimony, but He can't because the women are operating in carnality. Yes, Carnality! Your carnality can cause a delay in the blessings of God. Even a mature saint can be caught in this trap if she doesn't understand who Christ is. I'm not talking about the man who may force himself on a woman. We know this type of man is not ready for a wife, and the leadership of the Church should be told immediately.

I'm speaking on the woman enticing the man of God who has integrity, as Potiphar's wife attempted to entice Joseph in Genesis 39:7-10. *"And it came to pass after these things, that his master's wife cast her eyes upon Joseph; and she said, Lie with me. But he refused, and said unto his master's wife, Behold, my master wotteth not what is with me in the house, and he hath committed all that he hath to my hand; There is none greater in this house than I; neither hath he kept back any thing from me but thee, because thou art his wife: how then can I do this great wickedness, and sin against God? And it came to pass, as she spake to Joseph day by day, that he hearkened not unto her, to lie by her, or to be with her."*

Why do women carry themselves this way? Is it because you are wondering if he will ever see you in the midst of so many women? Here comes the power of God. The Lord puts it in a man's heart the woman he is to be with. The Lord doesn't decide based on your body, but your character. Women are often stronger when it comes to abstinence, so why don't you tell your flesh NO!? I believe it is because you are competing with other women. Some even think, "If I can get him hooked up, he'll have to be with me."

Consider what state of mind you are currently in. How do you really feel about other women? Are you in a bitter dispute with another woman? If the answer is yes, why is that? What's the true motive behind it? Is it a man or something material? Think for a moment. As a woman, what are you afraid of the most? Sometimes women only desire a certain man or certain material possessions because another woman has them. What is to be gained from this mindset?

Now answer this: How's your relationship with your mother, your sister, your daughter, your closest girlfriend? Can you trust them with your secrets? Can they trust you? To trust her to have your back in a fight is different than trusting her with a secret. Have you ever wondered why?

Think about it for a moment, we all know women who fit the descriptions above, some of us are included in that number, and no matter who we are the Lord loves us all. So, if God loves us all, why are there so many problems between women today? Some may casually say it's jealousy, and I believe jealousy is the root, but what is the soil that the root is growing in? Let's stop saying, "she's jealous," and let's deal with the problem.

Society has placed standards on women that cause us to hate one another. It's amazing the emphasis that is placed on appearance. The Lord declares in 1st Samuel 16:7 that He does not look on the outward appearance, but He looketh on the HEART. The heart, the very character of a woman, is not measured these days. Most of the time women are seen as trophies used to impress others. We all know that some of the most beautiful women in the world have the worst character. However, even in their worst state, the Lord Jesus loves them. Some women have gone through such trauma in their childhood that they are clearly messed up as adults, and we must remember, all trees, good and bad, have roots and soil.

We need to get to the root and the soil. The soil is the environment, upbringing, and surroundings. The soil nourishes the roots and branches of the tree. It's the Lord's desire that all of His children be set free from the power of the enemy. Whether the adversary has used society, childhood trauma, or something else; the Lord desires to bring forth deliverance and healing to the women that will be a part of His body. We have carried all the worldly issues between women into our relationship with Christ. The Church has been infiltrated with women's drama. It is a sad thing to have so many women at odds with each other, especially because of men. We are all made for a specific and special purpose. We don't have to compare ourselves with each other, so why do we do it?

It's actually insulting to the Lord, who created us all, to say one person is beautiful and another is not. No two women are exactly alike. We all have distinct differences. The differences in one woman are to complement the differences in other women. In Christ true beauty comes in many facets and has to do with the character. In Christ, we should celebrate the obedient, the holy, the righteous, the faithful, the meek and quiet, the virtuous, the humble, the modest, the truthful, and those that fear God with all their heart, not those with a beautiful appearance on the outside. The flesh will eventually age, fade, and pass away, but the true character of a woman will be with her for a lifetime.

I believe another problem is, as women, we don't know why God created us. When God reveals our purpose, we will be content with who we are and will be able to walk accordingly. We won't need to degrade other women to be accepted or to feel better about ourselves. We will come to love our sister in Christ and will soon learn that she can be an asset. We will come to respect each other's gifts, talents, and beauty when we really know who we are in Christ.

The way we feel about other women is a reflection of what we really are inside. Women have many different personalities and some may think or say, "Well my personality just clashes with hers," but our personality issues are not the root of many of our problems.

In the book of Deuteronomy 6:5, we are admonished to love the Lord with all our heart, soul, and might. Heart in this passage of Scripture is the seat (center) of emotions (Vines Dictionary). In Proverbs 23:12, the heart is the center of anything (S.C. 3820). Look at Proverbs 23:7. In this verse heart is the soul, life, self, the inner man (Vines Dictionary). Lastly, in Jeremiah 17:9-10, heart means the inner being of man, the man himself (S.C.), a man's heart is his very character.

"As such, the heart is the fountain of all man does. His thoughts, desires, words, and actions flow from deep within him. Yet a man cannot understand his own heart. As a man goes on in his own way, his heart becomes harder and harder, but God is able to circumcise - cut away the uncleanness of the heart of his people so that we will love and obey him with our whole being," (Deuteronomy 30:6) (Vines Dictionary).

Let's look at some biblical relationships between women and see the spirit, the heart, and the character behind their behavior, good or bad. Sarai and Hagar: Abrams wife and her Egyptian maid, Genesis 16:1-9. Hagar despised Sarai because she became pregnant with Abram's child and his wife Sarai had not conceived after decades. When the Bible declares Hagar despised Sarai, according to Strong's Concordance, it meant she brought her into contempt, she cursed her, she lightly esteemed her and she thought of herself as more. She made Sarai vile.

In the M.W.C.D. despise or despite means to look down on with contempt or aversion, to regard as negligible, worthless, and distasteful. Contemn implies a vehement condemnation of a person or thing as low, vile, or feeble. Many women today feel this way about other women in the Church. Remember I said in Chapter 8 that there was a woman that thought I was not good enough for my husband? She thought this and didn't even know me or what God had for me or the kind of woman my husband needed. She thought she should be the one with him without knowing what it would take to be with a man like him.

The world has put so much on women that when we come to the Lord, He has to take off many layers of mess. Oftentimes, He is unable to do this cleansing because we put on a façade like there is nothing going on with us. Too many women are operating in perpetration, pretense, and falsehood. Plainly, there are just too many women who do not like other women or think that other women do not like them. As long as we are hurting on the inside, we will continue to hurt other women.

The longer we hold on to things that hurt us we will not trust other women and the Lord will not be able to fully use us to build up His Kingdom. The more comfortable you are with who the Lord made you to be, the more you will love other women, and the more He can use you in His Kingdom.

Think about Miriam and Zipporah, Moses' sister and wife in Numbers 12:1 and 12:10. Miriam had a problem with Racism, which in the M.W.C.D. means, a belief that race is the primary determinant of human traits and capacities and that racial differences produce an inherent superiority of a particular race. Miriam believed the Hebrews were superior to the Ethiopians.

I believe the Lord punished Miriam and not Aaron because her motives were not right. And I believe her being a woman she spread gossip about Moses' wife in the camp amongst the women. Many Churches today cannot thrive the way the Lord would have it to because of this very reason. Imagine if God gave a man a wife of a different nationality. The women in the Church who were of the same nationality as the man would flip out. WHY? We are all supposed to be Christians! We are all God's children. The Lord is looking at the God you serve, not the color of your skin! It should not matter what color someone is. I believe a lot of people are going to be in for a surprise on judgment day due to this very issue.

And Leah and Rachel: Jacob's wives in Genesis 29:16-31 and 30:1-2, 8, 15, and 20 were envious of each other. Strong's Concordance defines envy as being zealous (eagerness and ardent interest in pursuit of something), jealous or envious, to be moved or provoked to jealousy. In the M.W.C.D. it means painful or resentful awareness of an advantage enjoyed by another joined with a desire to possess the same advantage. These two sisters were fighting over a shared husband. How many sisters today have slept with their sister's husband, boyfriend, or fiancé? Why would a sister breach her relationship with her sister for a man? Could Rachel have refused to marry Jacob since he was already married to Leah or could Leah have refused because Jacob loved Rachel?

What about Hannah, Elkanah's wife, in 1st Samuel 1:1-28? She experienced grief and torment at the hand of Peninnah. Grieved in the Hebrew definition, in Strong's Concordance, means to spoil, to make or be good for nothing, either psychologically, socially, or morally. And in the M.W.C.D. grieved means to cause to suffer distress, to feel grief, and sorrow. Torment in the M.W.C.D. means extreme pain or anguish of body or mind, agony. This is at the hand of another woman.

Consider Queen Vashti who lost her crown in Esther 1:3, 10-19. She refused to come before the king. I believe she was lifted with pride, became sick and tired of being a trophy, so she rebelled, which is the sin of witchcraft according to 1st Samuel 15:23a. The Hebrew definition for the word refused in Strong's Concordance means to refuse utterly (carried to the utmost point or highest degree).

In the M.W.C.D. it means to express oneself as unwilling to accept; to show or express unwillingness to do or comply with; deny; give up; or renounce. Rebellion in the M.W.C.D. means opposition to one in authority or dominance. Witchcraft in the M.W.C.D. means the use of sorcery or magic, communication with the devil or a familiar (spirit), an irresistible influence or fascination. Many women are operating in rebellion today and yet they are expecting a husband. Listen, God is not going to give you a man you can boss around.

The story of Naomi and Ruth, in the book of Ruth 1:16-18, 2:2, 11-12, 3:11, 4:13, is about a woman and her daughter-in-law, who in distress chose to care for one another. In the story, the Bible declares, Ruth was virtuous and the whole town knew it. The Hebrew definition for Virtuous in Strong's Concordance means a force: whether of men, means, or other resources. It means an army of wealth, virtue, valor, strength, able, activity, army, company, (great) forces, goods, host, might, power, riches, strength, strong, substance, train, valiant, valour, virtuous, war, and worthy. Virtuous in the M.W.C.D. means: potent, (having or wielding force, authority or influence), efficacious (having the power to produce the desired effect), having or exhibiting virtue, morally excellent, righteous, and chaste. We need more women like Ruth in the Body of Christ. And I mean with the laity. Ruth was not self-serving. If you are not willing to serve on the Lord's terms, you will have a miserable relationship with a husband because being married means you will be serving.

In the New Testament Jesus had many women followers, such as Mary Magdalene and others, Matthew 27:55-61, 28:1-10. The one thing they all had in common was faithfulness. They went to the cross with Jesus, when all His disciples, except for John the beloved, deserted Him. In the M.W.C.D. faithful is full of faith; steadfast in affection or allegiance, loyal, strong adherence to promises or in observance to duty. As Christian women, we should definitely be striving to be like these women. And we should be striving to love Christ and each other in at least the measure they did. Again, they went to the cross with Jesus. We have to have stronger character than many have these days. We have to be willing to suffer for righteousness' sake!

Queen Esther earned Vashti's crown, Esther 2:8-17. She exhibited the humility necessary for the position. The Bible declares she had the king's favor and was chosen above the rest. I believe this favor was due to the actual manifestation of her humility. The king didn't need just another beautiful face. He didn't need another Vashti. He needed someone with internal beauty. In the M.W.C.D. humility means the quality or state of being humble. Again, it was humility that the King and the men of his providence saw upon Esther, it was not her appearance. Vashti was beautiful, but the King was looking for something else in the new queen. Do you have the humility necessary for the Lord to choose you?

Remember Tabitha (Dorcas) the Humanitarian in Acts 9:36-41? She had done many good works and almsdeeds. The Greek definition for good in Strong's Concordance means good in any sense, benefit, good things, well. Works in Greek means to work; toil as an effort or occupation; act, deed, doing, labour, and work. Almsdeed in Greek means compassionateness as exercised toward the poor, beneficence (performing acts of kindness or charity).

In other words, she had good old fashion character, the character that many women despise today. Sometimes we say, "That was for my grandmother, that's not for me." But I'm telling you, we all need good old fashion character today. Tabitha (Dorcas) was not the kind of woman to take someone else's man or break up a happy home. This was the character of my husband's late mother Lillie. What a beautiful spirit Lillie had. She was really an example to me.

Then there were the holy women of old time as indicated in 1st Peter 3:1-6, *"Likewise, ye wives, be in subjection to your own husbands; that, if any obey not the word, they also may without the word be won by the conversation of the wives; While they behold your chaste conversation coupled with fear. Whose adorning let it not be that outward adorning of plaiting the hair, and of wearing of gold, or of putting on of apparel; But let it be the hidden man of the heart, in that which is not corruptible, even the ornament of a meek and quiet spirit, which is in the sight of God of great price. For after this manner in the old time the holy women also, who trusted in God, adorned themselves, being in subjection unto their own husbands: Even as Sarah obeyed Abraham, calling him lord: whose daughters ye are, as long as ye do well, and are not afraid with any amazement."*

These women adored and honored their husbands and knew what it meant to be in subjection to them. They had no problem with obedience. They were chase, meek, and quiet. In Strong's Concordance subjection means to be subordinate, to obey, be under obedience, and submit self to. Chaste means clean, innocence, modest, perfect, and pure. Meek means mild, humble, and meek. Quiet is keeping one's seat, stilled, undisturbed, peaceable, and quiet. I like the word quiet. In essence, it means, no matter what is going on, I am not moved, but I am at peace. In the M.W.C.D. subjection means to make oneself amenable (answerable) to the discipline and control of a superior (obedience is the act or instance of obeying). Can you believe this? Are you willing to be in subjection to your own husband?

Furthermore, chaste in the M.W.C.D. means pure in thought and action. This reminds me of 1st Corinthians 13:5d: love *"thinketh no evil."* Meek in the M.W.C.D. is enduring injury with patience and without resentment, mild (gentle). Finally, quiet is tranquility; easygoing temperament; enjoyed in peace and relaxation; free from noise or uproar; still; and unobtrusive. Oh, what the Body of Christ would be like if more of us women could display true meekness and quietness.

Now let's reflect. Look at Sarai and Hannah, women scorned because they *bear* no children, Sarai publicly and privately and Hannah by her adversary. Leah desired her husband's love and thought she could obtain it by having children; Rachel had her *husband's love* and felt worthless because she had no children. Zipporah, Moses' wife, was not accepted because of her race, and Vashti refused to be a trophy, so she rebelled.

In all of the negative examples, the women showed they had one thing in common. They needed acceptance. They needed to be loved. Christ is the <u>ONLY</u> one who can love us, as women, the way we need to be loved. He is LOVE! Therefore, true love can only and must first come from Him. When we abide in Christ and He abides in us, we will come to know His love, truly.

How do we do this? First, we must know, understand, and *walk-in* Scripture. Then we will come to love Christ in us and come to love ourselves. Then Christ will place opportunities in our lives to love other women. Then the rest is up to us to choose to love. Our deliverance will come the more we come to know and choose to surrender to Christ's love. Then we will no longer believe the evil reports that society, and those around us, teach and speak to us in regards to ourselves and other women.

The bottom line is this: all of mankind was birthed through women so the Lord must think highly of the woman. God is using the woman, by the power of the Holy Ghost, to sustain the body of Christ, and as long as the women in the Body of Christ are divided, the adversary will have succeeded in his plan to defeat many Churches and families.

I challenge each one of you to show love to other women, especially those that are of the household of faith. If you see a sister that doesn't have the right spirit, I challenge you to show her love. Don't talk about or alienate her, but love your sister by praying for her. Love is what women desire the most, and lots of it. Love starts with the condition of our own hearts. Love is one thing that will prevail when it is all said and done, 1st Corinthians 13:13, *"And now abideth faith, hope, charity, these three; but the greatest of these is charity."*

We have to remember that Love is what sent and kept Jesus on the cross. He died while we were yet sinners. That means in our worst state Jesus loved us. True love will cover our sister's sins. *"And above all things have fervent charity among yourselves: for charity shall cover the multitude of sins"* (1ˢᵗ *Peter 4:8).* As the children of God, we already have the victory, so let's walk in it and LOVE!

Chapter 10

Are You Prepared?

"I will therefore that the younger women marry, bear children, guide the house, give none occasion to the adversary to speak reproachfully."

1ˢᵗ Timothy 5:14

CHAPTER 10: ARE YOU PREPARED?

I believe there are some things that a woman should consider before she marries. In this chapter, I have made a list of questions and the real-life responses from a rap session I had in a women's meeting.

Many women waiting on husbands do not know what to expect. They wonder what their husband will be like and how marriage is going to be for them. Women often wonder what their husband will like or maybe not like about them. They wonder if he will like their personality or natural appearance. They may think, "How will he choose me from amongst so many women?"

Personally, I wondered how long it would be before he came for me. I pondered how cleaned up on the inside I would have to be in order for God to send him. A Christian girlfriend of mine, that was married years ago, once told me that some things about my character were not going to be brought to my attention until I actually married. She said, "These are things that you two will work on together." Sometimes, as women in the Church, we are afraid to ask these questions because we try not to appear unfocused, even though the questions press on our hearts often. I was really good at being single, and when my divine connection came, I found out I was terrible at being in a Godly relationship.

Again, when my husband arrived, I felt I was ill-prepared to be a wife. I never had a woman of God to share any of her personal experiences or struggles with me, nor did anyone tell me what it was really like being married as a Christian. For that reason, I am determined to share as much as I can to help women prepare so they will not be surprised.

These are the questions the ladies considered:

Q1. If you suddenly go from being single to married today, what drama would you bring to the table? This includes anything in your life that you would be ashamed for him to know about or you would be hesitant to tell him.

One of the responses was self-esteem issues. One woman said, *"If I don't feel I look beautiful and he says I'm beautiful, I could possibly attack him by saying, What do you mean I'm beautiful? You don't mean that. You're just trying to make me feel good about myself!"* Someone else said *she would think similar thoughts even though she wouldn't speak it. Another response was regarding the fluffy parts or wobbly bits of a woman's body. She would be ashamed to undress in front of him.*

If your husband starts making degrading comments about certain parts of your body, he needs serious prayer because no woman is perfect. And if she does have a really beautiful body, she may not think so. Personally, it was my feet that I didn't think were beautiful, but my husband says, "Your feet are marvelous." Later he told me, "You have beautiful teeth." Okay, I know he is sent from God.

Just remember the part you don't like may be the part he loves. Your divine connection will not see you the way you see yourself or the way others see you. Someone else said in the meeting, if you don't like something about yourself, change it. My counsel: Learn to love yourself the way you are before you start changing things and you will be a lot better off on the inside.

Q2. Where are your exes: husbands, baby's daddies, sex partners, boyfriends, etc.? Are they still pursuing you? Would they try to cause problems in your relationship to provoke your new spouse to anger or jealousy? Would "baby daddy" drama be an issue?

One woman said, *"Yes, my ex would try to purposely break up the relationship by any means."*

131

These ex-relationships have to be set in order before the new husband arrives to eliminate potential hindrances. Are you still pursuing your ex? Many women are still in love, lust, or are angry with their exes. The Lord can't send the person he has for you if you are still tied up with an old relationship. Forgive your ex and let him go physically, emotionally, and socially!

Q3. Who still cares for their ex? For example, if your ex died or were in the hospital would you be concerned or overwhelmed with grief? Someone said, *"Yes." They actually visited an ex in the hospital when he was sick.* Note: it wasn't to minister to him.

So, my question is if it were you who were married and he was concerned about his ex-wife or girlfriend and visiting her in the hospital how would you feel? The same person said they wouldn't care if the new husband went to see his ex because she doesn't think everyone is trying to get her man. I say to you, don't be foolish and naive to think you can totally trust another woman who used to be with your spouse. Besides, your new husband will not desire for you to have anything to do with your ex, even if he never says it.

I'm not saying be insecure and paranoid about your spouse. What I'm saying is many exes rekindle relationships because they never got over each other. And when you have any type of concern about an ex, they can emotionally manipulate you, again allowing themselves to be used by the enemy to cause a problem in your marriage. You have to remember that according to Ephesians 6:12, *"For we wrestle not against flesh and blood, but against principalities, against powers, against the rulers of the darkness of this world, against spiritual wickedness in high places."*

People have spirits that will war against your marriage. And if you care even a little about that ex, you will not let that relationship go if you were required to, by the Lord or your spouse. I know some of you have children with different individuals, however, you do not have to have a personal relationship with that person where you are talking about personal things or you are asking your children questions about the ex's life or lifestyle.

It's true that not everyone is going to try to rekindle an old flame, yet the devil likes stirring people up, and situations that would not normally take place could end up happening if you are not careful. Plus, when you are talking about a relationship that God ordained and put together, the enemy is going to fight tooth and nail to tear it apart and keep you at odds with each other and he will use exes to do it.

Another thing to consider: did you typically get a new man to get over another man? Why was that? Women do it to get distracted from the person they just broke up with. This is just another sign that you are not over your ex, and if you start a new relationship and haven't closed the door on the old one, it can mean disaster for your new relationship. **Don't trust flesh! Get over the exes completely!** If you don't get over your ex completely, the enemy may be successful in using this against your new marriage.

Q4. How is your prayer life? Not just do you pray, HOW is your prayer life? Are you consistent? Do you study the Bible? How is your praise? Do you know how to truly worship the Lord? Are you comfortable spending quality time alone in God's presence?

These things will not only make the difference in you being prepared for your husband, but they will also make a world of difference in keeping your husband and having a peaceful relationship. You and your spouse must both have a personal, obedient relationship with the Lord Jesus. That will keep the enemy out of your marriage.

Also, your husband will desire to have spiritual conversations with you. You two will share revelations of the Word and this will confirm your spirituality and relationship with the Lord to your spouse. No Godly man is going to listen to a woman gossiping or talking about a bunch of worldly mess. He will desire to hear the oracles of God, without you being too spiritual. Men like to hear their wives speak "sweet nothings" also.

My point is, if you don't have the Word of God in you, your conversation will be filled with junk. I'm not talking about you being able to repeat the things other people said about the Word of God, but I'm talking about actually having the Word of God in you. An unedifying conversation will minimize your level of spirituality in his eyes because he will know that you are worldly.

A lot of marriages don't work and it is becoming common for people to be married more than once. Your relationship with God has to be solidified and it should continue to grow even after you are married. This will ensure that you both are doing things God's way and not your own way. I remember when we got married, the Lord told my husband, "It's not going to go the way you think it should go, or the way she thinks it should go, but the way I say it will go." The Lord put His foot down, FLAT OUT!

Q5. Are you at peace when you are alone or would you rather be: shopping, on the phone, or at a movie? Can you be away from your children? Do you always feel like you have to be doing something?

This is the reason I ask. When people get in a relationship, sometimes, they get bored. One or both find themselves trying to entertain the other person and are never satisfied. That's one reason why people are going outside of the marriage because they are looking for something they can't find in their spouse. Their spouse doesn't have it, but they think they need it. And when they don't get it, oftentimes unfaithfulness steps in. They become dissatisfied in and with their relationship causing all kinds of problems and arguments. Then that person becomes boring to you.

My husband and I do not try to entertain each other. We enjoy the time the Lord allows us to have with each other, which is a lot. Not only do we still go on dates, we love taking drives in the car. We spend quiet time with each other or just shoot the breeze. We take naps together or just enjoy each other's presence while falling asleep. Neither of us has to be entertained, so when there is not a lot going on, we are not bored.

Q6. Are you content being single or do you feel you have to be married? If you feel you have to be married when do these feelings occur? Is it at a family gathering or when it would be convenient for you to have someone?

Most of the women said, "yes," they feel lonely when certain events at work or in the family are going on, which prompts the desire to be married. How long are you willing to wait on God for your divine connection? There are some women who are willing to marry anyone so they can be married. Some even get caught up in the vicious cycle of marrying, divorcing, and marrying again because they are not content being single and find it extremely difficult to wait on God.

Then there are the single women that will stay single rather than be married to the wrong person, but they will not be single and chaste. They are not willing to be single and walk in holiness while claiming to wait on God. They will fall into fornication while they are waiting, and think that is waiting. True waiting is doing it the Lord's way: chaste (meaning abstaining from sex on moral grounds) and not dating or fornicating!

Q7. What are you willing to give up for your marriage? Many people desire to be married, but they do not desire to give up anything. In a true Godly marriage, there is no place for selfishness. The more you both give up your desires and stop focusing on your own needs, the happier you both will be. God does mysterious things in your marriage when you stop thinking about yourself. Remember as Christians, we should all be striving to do what pleases the Lord and not what pleases our flesh.

Q8. Are you willing to change what you know about family life and your responsibilities in the household when your husband arrives? Someone said, *"I would not be willing to stay at home and be a housewife because if the man is doing everything, he could one day be angry and feel like what I am doing does not measure up to what he does."*

The truth of the matter is if you have a close personal relationship with the Lord Jesus, you will not find yourself marrying a man that is confused like that. And the Lord will not make you marry a man like that. Also, the woman should be content with guiding the house because it is declared in Scripture, 1ˢᵗ Timothy 5:14, *"I will therefore that the younger women marry, bear children, guide the house, give none occasion to the adversary to speak reproachfully."*

This declaration in Scripture does not mean we can't own a business, have a job, or go to school. Scriptures do not declare that we have to be "barefoot and pregnant." However, women should not have a problem being a housewife either.

Being a housewife and mother is one of the greatest duties a woman can have in this life. Besides, few have truly done it well. Maybe more women should strive to master it instead of abandoning it for a career. Furthermore, a truly Godly man, that fears the Lord, is not going to misunderstand or minimize the responsibilities the Lord has given the Christian wife. He will not devalue his bride lest he hinders his own prayers, 1st Peter 3:7, *"Likewise, ye husbands, dwell with them according to knowledge, giving honour unto the wife, as unto the weaker vessel, and as being heirs together of the grace of life; that your prayers be not hindered."* The Lord has a problem with men that mistreat their wives and He will fight on your behalf and correct your husband, as long as you are walking in the Word of God yourself.

Q9. Have you shown yourself faithful in not having sexual relationships with anyone since you have been saved? If not, understand that the Lord does not give faithful men of God to women that are not faithful while they are single in Christ. If you are whorish, you will not be getting a faithful man from the Lord. I'm not talking about when you come to Christ and you have to get over certain struggles. For some it may be "sticky fingers," and for others it may be fornication or lust. From the point of your deliverance have you been faithful to God? For some, the point of deliverance was at the time of confession. Unfortunately, many have strongholds that have to be dealt with over time. My point is: your level of faithfulness to Christ will determine the level of blessings you receive from the Lord.

Q10. Are you in the position to influence someone else to be Godly? This is important because God is placing you in the life of another person. Both of you will have to watch each other's back in the spirit realm. One could be going down the wrong road and someone has to be in a position to say, "No that is not what God is saying." Even if all you can do is pray that the Lord reveals the truth to your husband so he can make the right decision, you have to be in a position to know something is wrong.

It could be something as simple as looking for a house and you move into the wrong place and God's provision is not there because you two are not in His will. If this were to happen you would be in agreement with the decision because more than likely you were not able to discern when to agree and when not to agree with your husband, in the natural or in the spirit. I'm not saying to lead your husband; this is not the woman's place. You should be able to walk side by side with him and see something down the road that he may not be able to see. Just as you will not see everything and he may warn you.

Remember, when Pilate's wife in the Bible told him to have nothing to do with prosecuting Christ because she had received a warning in a dream? Matthew 27: 19, 24 *"When he was set down on the judgment seat, his wife sent unto him, saying, Have thou nothing to do with that just man: for I have suffered many things this day in a dream because of him."* Verse 24 was Pilate's response to the crowd based on what his wife told him: *"When Pilate saw that he could prevail nothing, but that rather a tumult was made, he took water, and washed his hands before the multitude, saying, I am innocent of the blood of this just person: see ye to it."*

As women, we have the power to influence and mislead our husbands down the wrong road if we are not walking in godliness. This is evident by the examples of Eve and Sarai in the Bible. This is something I can say about my husband: he listens to me because he knows I'm Godly. If you are raising hell all day, don't come in the evening and say, "The Lord said." Your husband is not going to hear you. If you are not in a position to influence someone else to be Godly and to make decisions that are according to the Lord's will, then you are not ready to be married.

Q11. Are you consistent in your temperament; your emotional temperature? As women, we have a lot of things that govern our temperament more than we govern our temperament. We have to learn to control our spirits. We should not be hot one minute and cold the next. We need to have an even, healthy temperament. Don't say that hormone imbalances in women are normal and don't ignore it like it's not a real issue. Pray that the Lord balances your hormones, especially around the time of your monthly cycle. He'll do it if you ask Him.

If you get angry and snap at other people then you will do it to your husband. If you get angry and hit someone else you will do it to your husband. What if your husband has a habit that you have a problem with? Are you going to act crazy trying to change him? You cannot act crazy if your husband does not do what you think he should be doing. You can't act crazy because a bill is not paid or he won't allow you to get a new cell phone.

Let go of the quirks you have about a lot of things that don't make a difference in life. Like: "Why did you put this dish in the sink without washing it; why is the toilet seat up; or why is your shirt on the floor?" Stop being lazy, be a wife, wash the dish, let the toilet seat down, pick up the shirt, and you will be a lot happier in life.

Be consistent in your temperament because the man of God is not going to contend with a woman that has a bad temperament. Men are not like women; they cannot take a whole lot of drama. Solomon wrote a lot about contentious women. In Proverbs 19:13b, he said, *"and the contentions of a wife are a continual dropping."* That is a continual drop of water according to Proverbs 27:15, *"A continual dropping in a very rainy day and a contentious woman are alike."* Dripping water is irritating! And can cause a lot of damage over time.

Additionally, King Solomon wrote that he'd rather be in a tiny room with peace than in a large house with a brawling woman, *(Proverbs 21:9 and 25:24)*. He also said, *"It is better to dwell in the wilderness, than with a contentious and an angry woman,"* *(Proverbs 21:19)*. I think we should take Solomon's counsel because he had 700 wives and 300 concubines, 1st Kings 11:3. Your nagging is one sure thing that will ruin your marriage and there will be no one to blame but **yourself!**

If you are a person that is up and down all the time in your temperament, ask the Lord why and then ask for deliverance. The Bible declares, *"He that hath no rule over his OWN spirit is like a city that is broken down, and without walls,"* *(Proverbs 25:28)*. This means you are exposed to all possible attacks of the enemy.

Q12. If God puts extreme pressure on you, what will come out? Is it filthy communication? *One of the ladies said rage!* This is a sign that she needs prayer and some serious deliverance and should ask the Lord to take that away from her before she enters a marriage. Rage is not for the marriage covenant because there will be times you will disagree, especially in the beginning during the adjustment

144

period, and if you can't control your emotions without being wrathful, someone may get hurt, emotionally, mentally, or physically.

Another sister said when she was under extreme pressure she just yelled, *"Why, God Why!?" Then she began to praise the Lord. Someone else said, "When I first got saved, I went through the changes of yelling, but then I started to pray and was able to get through the situation."*

It's good to let off steam, but don't subject another person to it, remember steam burns. The Lord can take it, but other people may not be able to. I will also advise that you be careful how you talk to the Lord because saying the wrong thing to him can also get you into big trouble. You have to know what's on the inside of you and get rid of those things that are not balanced before your husband arrives.

Q13. When you "get real," are you still Godly? When you get real that means the façade goes. Façade in the M.W.C.D. means a false, superficial, or artificial appearance. Everyone has a side of them that "gets real." You have to know yourself. No one else should know more about you than you. Some people don't ask God to remove things from them because they don't know to ask. One true sign of us getting real is how we treat our children. Many parents think they have a license to mistreat their children. Some of you may have heard the saying, "I brought you into this world, and I'll take you out." You do not have the right to kill your children; so, stop saying it. Or when we get angry, we let all kinds of evil words spill from our mouths. The sad thing is that after you 'get real', the dust settles, and you think you feel better because you got a lot of things off your chest. However, the truth is a lot of people are left hurting because you didn't know how to settle issues peaceably.

Usually after you 'get real' you're faced with a bunch of sad spirits who are dealing with what you said, as you try to say you didn't mean it and insincerely ask for forgiveness. We have to be careful about what we speak out of our mouths because the truth is, once it is said, you can't clean it up or take it back, no matter how much time passes. Ideally, we should be able to, but we are humans with real feelings and emotions so it's hard to forget things people said or did to us when they were angry. Besides, the Bible declares in Matthew 12:34e, *"for out of the abundance of the heart the mouth speaketh."* If you said it, more than likely you meant it.

The Word of God also declares in Hebrews 12:14-15 that we must, *"Follow peace with all men, and holiness, without which no man shall see the Lord: Looking diligently lest any man fail of the grace of God; lest any root of bitterness springing up trouble you, and thereby many be defiled;"* Many Christians are defiled with bitterness and they wonder why no one desires to be around them. It's hard to commune with a bitter and angry, unforgiving person who is always trying to give someone a piece of their mind. If you are like this, you are surely going to ruin your marriage and many personal relationships. I know several people that have ruined relationships with other people because of outbursts or they just had to tell everyone how they felt. Then they ask for forgiveness and think that everything is supposed to go back to normal.

The bottom line is it is not good to store up anger for a rainy day. The Word declares, *"Be ye angry, and sin not: let not the sun go down upon your wrath: Neither give place to the devil. . . . Let no corrupt communication proceed out of your mouth, but that which is good to the use of edifying, that it may minister grace unto the hearers. And grieve not the holy Spirit of God, whereby ye are sealed unto the day of redemption. Let all bitterness, and wrath, and anger, and clamour, and evil speaking, be put away from you, with all malice: And be ye kind one to another, tenderhearted, forgiving one another, even as God for Christ's sake hath forgiven you" (Ephesians 4:26-27, 29-32).* Please understand that when you cause people a lot of pain, they may forgive you and move on without you. There are just some people who are not going to stick around for you to hurt them again, especially if you have a history of doing it over and over. And, if that person is required to follow peace with all men, sometimes peace will only be maintained at a distance.

It is your duty to get matters settled before the day expires. The key thing to remember when getting issues settled is both people, or everyone involved, has to be open to getting the matter settled, as well as forgiving each other. My husband and I have a rule: get the issue straightened out before we go to sleep. If either of us allows an issue to linger we conclude it is not an issue because no one brought it up. If someone waits until the next day, that person is wrong because that matter should have been dealt with yesterday. Every night we get on our knees together and pray before going to bed, so if there was something that needed to be cleared up, it should have been done prior to prayer. Yesterday is done and over. Besides, it would be a terrible thing for you to go to sleep angry and go into judgment with a lot of unresolved mess. The point is for you to know your own flaws and learn how to settle matters peaceably.

Q14. For those who have been married before, what went wrong in your marriage? One person said, *"My husband's ex-girlfriend and my ex-boyfriend were able to aggressively cause distrust between us."* Another person mentioned, *"Everything was fine in the beginning, but then he began to verbally abuse me."* A third person remarked, *"He cheated and physically abused me."* Someone else commented, *"My mother-in-law continued to interfere with my marriage, instructing my husband and constantly contradicting the Godly counsel I gave as the wife."*

In the latter case, if he would have taken hold of one Scripture, Genesis 2:24, *"Therefore shall a man leave his father and his mother, and shall cleave unto his wife: and they shall be one flesh,"* it could have possibly saved their marriage.

It is good to know what you did wrong in your last marriage to make sure you don't do the same thing again and ruin the blessing the Lord has for you. Don't just consider what the other person did, consider what you did wrong and correct yourself. If you desire something new and wonderful in your new marriage, you have to do something different for it to be wonderful because the common factor

in both marriages will be you.

Chapter 11

How Did I Know He Was the One?

"Howbeit when he, the Spirit of truth, is come, he will guide you into all truth: for he shall not speak of himself; but whatsoever he shall hear, that shall he speak: and he will shew you things to come."

John 16:13

CHAPTER 11: HOW DID I KNOW HE WAS THE ONE?

First, I will say, don't let anyone talk to you about the spouse the Lord is sending you, because many of you waited a long time to be blessed. So, don't mess up your blessing by jumping on a gossip bandwagon about the very person you are supposed to marry. Actually, you should not be talking about anyone because you never know who is to be your husband and gossip is displeasing to the Lord.

We were always taught by our spiritual leaders that if the person is not the one, you will have a "check" in your spirit. I understood just what this meant. Before I was saved, I always knew that the different men I was involved with were not for me to marry. For example, there was one person whom I trusted, but I knew deep inside he was not faithful.

When the truth came out, I was devastated; but as I said, I knew all along something was not right, I just didn't desire to face the truth. Then there was another person whom I was with that I knew was selfish and that if I ever married him, I'd be unhappy because he would always put his needs above mine. These are just a couple of examples of "checks" in my spirit about different men and when I got saved it didn't change, it increased. I believe the Lord has given this to most people so they will know those who are not right for them. If you heed the "checks" the Lord gives you in your spirit, you will not miss the spouse the Lord has for you, especially if you have the Holy Ghost.

After my divine connection and I were dating for a while, we both really began to fast and pray to be sure we were supposed to take the relationship to the next level and get married. During this time, the Lord kept confirming to us inwardly and outwardly that we were to marry. Literally, everywhere we went, we were told that the Lord desired for us to marry. We would smile and say, "We know." People we didn't really know were asking us to invite them to our wedding. It was so strange, but we knew it was the Lord. There were also a lot of people saying we looked like brother and sister. We were constantly getting confirmations from strangers. It was blessed to have the Lord making it so plain for us so we would not miss Him.

Although the enemy was trying to use my naivety and preconceived ideas of what he was to be like against me, the Lord was intervening to make sure I didn't miss it. The only true way to know is to continue to fast and pray until the Lord emphatically reveals it to you because you shouldn't marry someone based on what someone else says. You have to know for yourself. It's the same way if you have been called to ministry. You can't step out into ministry based on what your Pastor or momma said. You have to know for yourself because when the enemy comes to try you and your marriage or ministry, you will only be able to stand on what the Lord told you, not what He told someone else.

You can't depend on a dream, a prophecy, or even the other person because many times the message given will only be part of the big picture and may seem more like a mystery than a message. You have to know for yourself. Don't look for signs and flashing lights, because if one is given, it may not be God. It could be the enemy trying to set you up to keep you from fulfilling the call on your life.

Women may even have personal signs that they are expecting the man to show that are supposed to give them a clue that he is the man the Lord is sending to be their husband. For example, women say, "He has to be the one because he is good with children or he does good work around the house." Yes, it may be that he is willing to work for you as Jacob worked for Rachel in the book of Genesis. However, is he to be your husband? Is he even capable of being a husband? A lot of men can do yard work, but that does not make him a husband, or the man the Lord has ordained for you.

You may say, "Well, he helps me out when I need something." That's good, but is he your husband? Has the Lord told you he is to be your husband? Have you objectively listened and considered what other people are saying about him? Do they see something in him that you are refusing to admit, but you know is true? See it's one thing for people to be jealous and only see negative things, and it's another thing for you to see the same thing they see, know it's true, and are too prideful to admit it.

People were saying a lot of things about my spouse-to-be, but they didn't even know him. I spent time with him, so I knew the truth. Not only that, I had warnings from the Lord of what the enemy was going to try to do and say before it happened. So, when it did, I was not surprised. Besides, the Lord had shown me personally what He was going to do in him. Most humans have an innate ability to only see the negative side of people. They don't care if they are seeing the hurt someone else may have caused this person or not. All they see is negativity. They don't see a person's potential. I have found that most humans do not desire for you to be happier than they are. It's okay if you do well, but just don't do better than they are doing. So, I have learned to listen to the Lord rather than people.

You will even have to be careful of people you trust saying the Lord told them this and that about the spouse the Lord is sending you. One person lied and told me the Lord told her we were having sex. She told me she talked to other people about it and they told her the Lord told them the same thing. I thought it was funny because she was in sexual sin at the time. As a matter of fact, she was in sexual sin from the beginning of her walk with the Lord. I have learned that people have what I call "mirror syndrome." They will see in your spouse what they are. If they are unholy and lustful, they will suddenly see it in your spouse to be. They will assume you are doing what they are doing in relationships. Some people have ruined their own Christian testimony, so they will try to ruin yours. Be careful of who you trust and call a friend. Proverbs 16:28 declares, *"A froward man soweth strife: and a whisperer separateth chief friends."*

These are the same people who will not pray but they will tell everyone they know what they claim the Lord told them. The Lord is not a liar or a gossiper. He does not share secrets with people that have diarrhea of the mouth. The Bible declares in Proverbs 11:13, *"A talebearer revealeth secrets: but he that is of a faithful spirit concealeth the matter."* The Lord shares things with those that are of a faithful spirit because He knows they will pray and not gossip. Furthermore, Proverbs 11:9 declares, *"An hypocrite with his mouth destroyeth his neighbour: but through knowledge shall the just be delivered."*

There was another person that I met that was encouraging me on the one hand and trying to give me so called "words of the Lord" on the other hand, while all along she didn't like my future husband. One time she was saying we were supposed to be together and at other times she was saying something contrary. Listen, you cannot prophesy to or about someone you have a problem with because you will only see that which is negative. Just because you put the Lord's name on it doesn't make it true. All the gifts of the Spirit operate on the principle of love. 1st Corinthians 13:2 declares, *"And though I have the gift of prophecy, and understand all mysteries, and all knowledge; and though I have all faith, so that I could remove mountains, and have not charity (love - S.C. 26), I am nothing."*

Also, if the person who is trying to minister to you is not right in their spirit or has had some bad experiences with men, relationships, or marriage, they are going to think everyone is like what they have experienced and will be speaking to you out of fear. I had a person like this trying to minister to me. She was actually trying to convince me subtly not to marry my divine connection because she thought he was like her ex-husband. She had a form of the "mirror syndrome." Everything she was telling me was based on what she experienced in her last marriage, yet she still believed the Lord was going to send her a third husband. I'm convinced that women like this will counsel others to wait until some "perfect man" comes along before they get married, but this very same person will marry the first man that smiles at them and no one would be able to convince her otherwise.

A specific example of this "mirror syndrome" happened when I was in the choir and one of the minstrels that listened to secular music, accused the whole choir of listening to secular music. He thought that we all were in the same boat as he. He even went as far as saying he wouldn't believe us if we told him otherwise. The truth was: many of us only listened to Gospel music and because he lived a different lifestyle, he assumed we were all living the same way. It's the same line as "all men cheat" or "all women cheat." People who say this are usually cheaters! When I used to hear this saying, before I was saved, I knew it wasn't true because I didn't cheat or show myself to be untrustworthy in a relationship. I knew there were some men out there in the world that didn't cheat because I knew I was a woman who didn't. *"And if any man think that he knoweth any thing, he knoweth nothing yet as he ought to know" (1ˢᵗ Corinthians 8:2).*

I have found that Christians who are not able to refrain from sexual sin, are the main ones who assume others can't. They often accuse others to make themselves feel better. If it is someone you trust that is accusing you or spreading gossip, you should truly consider how important that relationship is to you because more than likely this person does not have your best interest at heart.

Matthew 7:1-5 declares, *"Judge not, that ye be not judged. For with what judgment ye judge, ye shall be judged: and with what measure ye mete, it shall be measured to you again. And why beholdest thou the mote that is in thy brother's eye, but <u>considerest not the beam that is in thine own eye</u>? Or how wilt thou say to thy brother, Let me pull out the mote out of thine eye; and, behold, a beam is in thine own eye? Thou hypocrite, first cast out the beam out of thine own eye; and then shalt thou see clearly to cast out the mote*

160

out of thy brother's eye. According to Strong's Concordance, Mote (2595) in this passage of Scripture is a dry twig or straw; and a Beam (1385) is a stick of timber. I think of these accusers as people walking around with a tree log in their eye tearing up everything in their path.

No one else should know your potential spouse better than you do if you have spent time with that person. You should have your eyes open to see and receive the truth the Lord will show you about a person while you are dating them. Don't start dating someone and get all goo-goo-eyed that you can't see the truth. People thought this is what happened to me, but it wasn't. The Lord was telling us both: the good, the bad, and the ugly about each other and we chose to work through it all together.

We both had hurts from the past that needed to be worked through. We both needed deliverance from these hurts. We realized that we were not the ones who hurt each other, and we were put together so the Lord could heal us together and use these very experiences to minister to others. I knew exactly what I was doing because the Lord was leading me every step of the way in my situation. And now that we are married, we are very in love and happy. Our marriage is full of peace, joy, and understanding and the people around us know it.

You may not see beams of light, hear fireworks or bells ringing, but when your spouse comes, you are going to know it if you ask the Lord. Make sure you keep your heart open for a NO he is not the one! If you already have your mind made up regardless of what the Lord has to say, you may not get to know the truth until it's too late. The bottom line is prayer, fasting, humility, and an open heart is the only true way to hear from God.

Chapter 12

Maximum Temptation

"It is good for a man not to touch a woman."

1ˢᵗ Corinthians 7:1b

CHAPTER 12: MAXIMUM TEMPTATION

I had just moved into a new home and was excited about what the Lord was getting ready to do in my life. Two weeks after the move, I had a dream that I was going to lose my home. I had this same dream a few times over the next few months. The focus of each dream was that when I lost my home, I was not going to have a place to stay. My sons and I were wandering from place to place with nowhere to go. I never told anyone about my dreams because I thought if I didn't speak about them, I could pray against them and keep them from coming to pass.

Later, I came to understand that the Lord was all in it. I was about to embark on an experience that would change my life for the good. It was the Lord's way of preparing me for the next level in ministry. The calling on my life required that I go through a serious trial for the next level of anointing. A lot of people have great callings and are not willing to go through what is necessary to fulfill them. Many are concerned about their reputations, friendships, family, finances, careers, and material possessions. They will not give up their lifestyles, even if it is mediocre.

Mark 10:28-30 declares, *"Then Peter began to say unto him, Lo, we have left all, and have followed thee. And Jesus answered and said, Verily I say unto you, There is no man that hath left house, or brethren, or sisters, or father, or mother, or wife, or children, or lands, for my sake, and the gospel's, But he shall receive an hundredfold now in this time, houses, and brethren, and sisters, and mothers, and children, and lands, with persecutions; and in the world to come eternal life.*

I'm not going to defend myself and say that we were not having sex, even though we were not, because you all wouldn't believe me anyway. So, I won't waste time writing a defense for something the reader didn't live and won't believe. The truth is we had a strong attraction for one another. We needed the power of the Holy Ghost to keep and restrain us. In the beginning, it wasn't easy, but the Lord said to him one day, "This too shall pass." I learned through this process that what I did as a single person to keep from falling was not going to work while waiting to be married.

As a single person, I cut off all communication with men, period! So, when my divine connection finally came, I had no clue of what to do. We did fast and pray and that was not enough, because

166

when we did see each other, the natural chemistry we were trying to suppress arose once again. We had to get busy doing work on my new, un-groomed home or the enemy would have used the natural attraction we had for one another to cause us to fall into sin, ultimately making some babies out of wedlock. It's true!

If you don't subdue your flesh you will fall into sin. I remember the Lord distinctly telling me, "If you have sex with him, you will surely conceive." I was shocked! It was during this time that the Lord spoke to me and said that intercourse is like entering the court and is worship between a husband and a wife, which we were not. What were we to do? We couldn't hide from one another, and you can't get to know someone with a whole lot of other people around, so the Lord gave us a project.

My new spouse to be, came up with a plan, at the Lord's command, to complete the necessary work on my new home. He spent 12-hour days in the hot sun, pulling up weeds, trenching, hoeing, laying a sprinkler system that he designed, plumbing, laying sod, painting the house, laying landscaping bricks and paver stones, putting a sink in the basement, mounting and wiring a garage door opener, and wallpapering the kitchen. My neighbors witnessed this hardworking man and began to walk by my house to compliment the work that he was doing, all professionally done at no charge.

The Lord was showing me his work ethic and that he was a man of his word. I also saw that he had been given a Spirit of Excellence from the Lord. Anyone who really knows him knows that he is a man of superb skill, knowledge, and abilities. I was impressed! He is definitely a proper, old-school gentleman. I love this about him. At this time, about five months of dating, a leader in the Church, who really is a Prophet, told me it would be at least three years before we married. I said, "Three years? I plan on getting married before that!" Well, the word of the Lord was true; it was another three years before we were married.

While we were dating, it was revealed to me that many saints that meet their divine connection will not be honest about the struggles they went through prior to marriage because humans are judgmental. The truth is that many are not having intercourse, but there are a lot of substitutions going on. Many are doing what the world does to satisfy the urges of the flesh. Rubbing, touching, delighting in sexual dreams, and even masturbation. I remember someone telling me that it was okay to have dreams of having sex and that it was not a sin. The devil is a liar!

I know someone else who desired those dreams. She told me, "I love when I have dreams about having sex. It's not wrong." And someone else told me, "You know how far you can go. It's okay to kiss and touch." I don't know about her, but for me kissing alone was too much. I'd be trying to go all the way just from a peck on the cheek. A man's touch is powerful. *"It is good for a man not to touch a woman. Nevertheless, to avoid fornication," (1ˢᵗ Corinthians 7:1b, 7:2a-b).* If you are avoiding fornication, don't touch!

I know two women who are saved and have been married at least six times between the two of them. They both said, "**All men will ask to try it once before marriage.**" I was shocked! I concluded that there are not enough married Christians telling the truth about their dating experiences. In this conversation, they told me what some of the men they dated said to them: "Just let me stick the head in. It's okay, we're getting married anyway. I would like to know what I'm getting before I get married." Yeah right! If you let him "stick the head in," you will be riding the whole shaft. Yes, I said it! The whole shaft! I hear someone saying right now, "Oh my God, is she really saved?" Yes, I am! I'm not writing this book to put on airs, but to uncover the devil's plan.

The bottom line is those who don't have this struggle are either not attracted to each other or they are those who get married so fast that the door to the enemy is closed, even according to Scripture. They choose not to wait, burning with uncontrollable passion. Besides ladies, after he gets a piece of your goodies, he will leave talking about he's looking for a saved sister. 1st Corinthians 7:9 declares, *"But if they cannot contain, let them marry: for it is better to marry than to burn."* For those of us whom the Lord will not allow to marry quickly, we have to rely on fasting and prayer to get us through this time. Make yourself productive doing the Lord's business.

Personally, I desired to be attracted to my divine connection. I didn't have a list of things I was expecting in my mate, but I did ask the Lord to give me a husband that would be obedient to Him, regardless of what man was saying, and I also asked that we would please each other in the bed-chamber once we were married. If there is no attraction between a man and a woman prior to the marriage, I believe the enemy will use this to attack the couple once they are married. I know there are couples that have not consummated their marriages after several years because they are not attracted to each other. I'm not talking about lusting after someone; however, I'm talking about being pleased with the way the person looks, dresses, and carries him or herself. I'm talking about a stirring or excitement you feel in your spirit when you are around them. Not a lust in your loins or lower parts.

I believe each believer will be attracted to a true divine connection. Yes, I know about the shallow believers which have rejected their divine connections because of their teeth, hair loss, weight, etc. I'm speaking on the majority of Christians that meet someone and think it's a sin to be attracted to that person physically. If you marry someone you are not attracted to, I believe the enemy will be able to breach your marriage sooner or later.

In my situation, I did a lot of fighting with my flesh when my divine connection arrived because when I was in the world, I liked having sex. However, while dating in Christ I could not carry myself that way. I didn't know how to date and I didn't desire to date in groups. My attitude was: I've waited so long that I'm going to enjoy my time getting to know this person. People can be phony when other people are around, but when you are by yourselves the truth will come out. Besides, so many people were jealous of my blessing that I couldn't find anyone who was genuine about the situation to date with us in a group.

Keep in mind that I hadn't had a date in six years. I was so excited I didn't know what to do. I remember someone telling me about a homemaking class they took at the Church. A female instructor said, "I'm not marrying anyone that I haven't kissed." That sounds like kissing is okay; and for her, it may have been, yet for me, that was giving me permission to have sex and I knew this. The truth is a person can be sexually aroused just from kissing because everyone's sex drive is different. You have to know what to do with all those emotions.

Now that we are married, it makes marriage much more pleasurable and when the enemy tries to come in, he can't because we are constantly showing each other affection in many ways, including keeping open lines of communication, ensuring there are no breaches in our union that he can penetrate. Unless it's that forbidden time, we make sure we are having sex as often as possible.

The maximum temptation came in when I became homeless and had nowhere to go. After two and a half years, I had to leave my new home. The doors were shut by God. People were saying I could have moved in with family, but some family members were saying the Lord told them not to help me. I believe he did turn their heart from assisting me. Besides, after you have been on your own for nearly twenty years, it's hard to go back to living with family members. Especially, when you have family that will throw things up in your face that they do for you or say to you every day, get a job; I'm not taking care of a grown person.

Also, you can't live with people who do not understand what the Lord is doing in your life. So, moving in with family was not an option for me. My divine connection and his mother, God rest her soul, took me and my two sons in at the expense of their reputations, until the Lord could lead me in what to do next. We all went on a seven-day fast and on the seventh day, we all were set out on the street in the cold. Yes, his mom lost her home a week after I moved in. She was going through her own trial at the same time I was and we didn't even know each other. She moved into her home the same month and year that I did and lost it at the same time and she was a woman that had been employed by the same employer for nearly forty years and had excellent credit.

When we were evicted from my future mother-in-law's home, it was January, about 16 degrees Fahrenheit, snowing, and getting colder as the evening drew near. While the moving truck was being loaded with his mother's things, people in the neighborhood were riding by to see what they could take for themselves, so we couldn't leave anything and come back. My future spouse had to stay with the truck. We were outside now for seven hours in the cold. By this time my sons were getting in and out of the car to stay warm and my future husband continued to load the van without a break from the cold, like a man on a mission.

I have never seen a man work this hard and long in the cold. We were getting hungry and again we were extremely cold. I kept getting out of the car to help him with his mother's things because I couldn't stand to see him working by himself. His mother sat in the car with my sons. As he continued to load the truck, we went to the gas station to put some gas in the car. While there, we saw a man looking for food in the trash. My youngest son, who was thirteen years old, said, "Give him something," so we gave him a little money to get something to eat and returned to the house. When we got back, he was done loading the van.

This is a man who had just moved from another country. When he came back to America, his mother was not walking fully with the Lord, so this trial was to secure her salvation and to solidify mine and prepare me for ministry. The evening we were evicted, my future spouse asked me and his mother, where did we desire to go? We told him emphatically, "We're going with you." It's easy for a man to move on and survive without two women and two children to be concerned with, but he wasn't thinking about himself, nor was any of us thinking about what others would say. We were homeless.

It took us three days to find somewhere stable to go. The first night we stayed in a motel where prostitution was running rampant. The place was so filthy it was ridiculous, yet we appreciated it because it was a place to lay our heads inside from the cold. And the second night we slept in the car outside of the storage facility where we stored our things. On the third day, it was snowing like crazy and we were driving around hungry, dirty, tired, and freezing cold trying to determine our next move. After paying for the moving truck and the storage facility, we had a total of $63 left between the three of us and a trunk load of meats we had just purchased that were vacuum wrapped three days before and still frozen.

Then the Lord said to drive in a certain direction and turn here, and there, and we drove past an Extended Stay. I said, "We should go back." When we went back the manager welcomed us and we saw the room, which was clean and had a kitchenette. We knew we could stay there a couple of days, which actually turned out to be two years. The Lord showed himself to be mighty and provided for us the entire time we were there.

When people found out the situation we were in, they immediately began to throw stones. The rumors were flying and the saints were the main source of gossip, including some so-called ministers. Many spiritual leaders do not see themselves as self-righteous, but they are. Just because a well-known spiritual leader says something about a situation and puts the Lord's name on it, that doesn't make it true. The thing is, while everyone said we were living together, we saw it as surviving together. The time we spent in that room was the most difficult time I had to face in my life. I was not used to any type of suffering like that. It was like being in military basic training for two years. After the first 8 months, I got to the point where I didn't care what people thought of me because after the Lord closed every door, I knew I was one step away from being homeless. I knew I was not to run to my family for assistance, *"neither go into thy brother's house in the day of thy calamity: for better is a neighbor that is near than a brother far off"* (Proverbs 27:10d-e).

If you've never been homeless in Christ, don't tell me what you wouldn't do. I found out personally, what I put my mouth on years before, I was experiencing, and it was worse. I now understand that the Lord can do what He desires in the lives of his children and they don't have to be backslidden. What did we do to not fall into sin? We continued to fast and pray like crazy and ministered to a lot of souls.

Initially, after moving in, I cried for six months. People were treating me so badly it was very depressing. We desired to be in the Lord's will, so, I continued to pray the Lord would open a door for me to find a place to stay. He didn't and He finally told me that I was already in His will. I thought within myself, "Lord you are going to have to give me Scripture." Immediately, Jacob, Leah, and Rachel, in Genesis 29:16-19, came to me. *"And Laban had two daughters: the name of the elder was Leah, and the name of the younger Rachel. Leah was tender eyed; but Rachel was beautiful and well favoured. And Jacob loved Rachel; and said, I will serve thee seven years for*

Rachel thy younger daughter. And Laban said, It is better that I give her to thee, than that I should give her to another man: <u>abide with me</u>." This is how I saw my relationship with him. He worked untiringly for me.

Then Moses and Zipporah, in Exodus 2:16-21, came to me. *"Now the priest of Midian had seven daughters: and they came and drew water, and filled the troughs to water their father's flock. And the shepherds came and drove them away: but Moses stood up and helped them, and watered their flock. And when they came to Reuel their father, he said, How is it that ye are come so soon to day? And they said, An Egyptian delivered us out of the hand of the shepherds, and also drew water enough for us, and watered the flock. And he said unto his daughters, And where is he? why is it that ye have left the man? call him, that he may eat bread. And Moses was content to <u>dwell with the man:</u> and he gave Moses Zipporah his daughter.*

Finally, Joseph and Mary rushed to my mind. *"And in the sixth month the angel Gabriel was sent from God unto a city of Galilee, named Nazareth, To a virgin <u>espoused to a man</u> whose name was Joseph, of the house of David and the virgin's name was Mary,"* (Luke 1:26-27). *"And it came to pass in those days, that there went* *out a decree from Caesar Augustus, that all the world should be taxed. (And this taxing was first made when Cyrenius was governor of Syria.) And all went to be taxed, every one into his own city. And Joseph also went up from Galilee, out of the city of Nazareth, into Judaea, unto the city of David, which is called Bethlehem; (because he was of the house and lineage of David:) To be taxed <u>with Mary</u> his <u>espoused wife</u>, being great with child."* Luke 2:1-5. *"Now the birth of Jesus Christ was on this wise: When as his mother Mary <u>was espoused to Joseph, before they came together,</u> she was found with child of the Holy Ghost. Then Joseph her husband, being a just man, and not willing to make her a publick example, was minded to put her away privily"* Matthew 1:18-19. Mary was with Joseph, abiding and traveling with him and they were yet espoused. I can only imagine all the self-righteous people talking about Mary and Joseph.

Let me say, that I am not comparing myself directly with any of these women, and I know historically that Jacob and Moses would have dwelled in separate tents from the women, yet it was clear to me that all these men were <u>dwelling</u> with their espoused wives before there was a marriage. Dwelling in the [M.W.C.D. means to remain for a time; to live as a resident; a shelter (as a house) in which people live.] After the Lord brought these Scriptures to mind, a supernatural peace came over me because I had been previously told, a year earlier, by my future husband that the Lord said we were espoused (S.C. 3423), which means *betroth* in Strong's Concordance and *to promise to marry* in the Merriam-Webster Collegiate Dictionary. To confirm that we were all in the Lord's will, the Lord had a seasoned Prophetess out of Georgia, who didn't know us and who had never met us, tell my husband the Lord said not to leave the room and everyone who was with him was to stay will him or we would hurt ourselves.

However, in all this, the Lord cautioned me that my liberty in Him could be a stumbling block for someone else; so, we had to continue admonishing people to marry and abstain from fornication, before living together, and not feel like people were going to call us hypocrites because we were in a precarious situation. *"But take heed lest by any means this liberty of yours become a stumblingblock to them that are weak. And through thy knowledge shall the weak brother perish, for whom Christ died" (1ˢᵗ Corinthians 8:9, 11)?*

People have a tendency to judge other people's situations based on what they would do, not realizing the Lord will put us through things that others will not understand. And believe me; I know what the Scripture reads in 1st Thessalonians 5:22, *"Abstain from all appearance of evil."* I personally know that everything that appears to be evil is not evil. I remember once the Lord told me: "The next time someone judges you concerning your situation, ask them this question: The suffering of Job; was it for righteousness' sake or his sin?"

"And said, Naked came I out of my mother's womb, and naked shall I return thither: the Lord gave, and the Lord hath taken away; blessed be the name of the Lord. In all this Job sinned not, nor charged God foolishly" (Job 1: 21-22). "But he said unto her, Thou speakest as one of the foolish women speaketh. What? shall we receive good at the hand of God, and shall we not receive evil? In all this did not Job sin with his lips" (Job 2:10-11).

Chapter 13

Miserable Comforters are ye!

"I have heard many such things: miserable comforters are ye all."

Job 16:2

CHAPTER 13: MISERABLE COMFORTERS ARE YE!

"There is none that understandeth, there is none that seeketh after God. They are all gone out of the way, they are together become unprofitable; there is none that doeth good, no, not one. Their throat is an open sepulcher; with their tongues they have used deceit; the poison of asps is under their lips: Whose mouth is full of cursing and bitterness: Their feet are swift to shed blood: Destruction and misery are in their ways" (Romans 3:11-16).

While we were in "The Room," a 20' x 12' (l x w) rectangle, the Lord was sending strangers to encourage us. These were individuals from other ministries who didn't know us and who hadn't been told a bunch of lies about our situation. We also visited several ministries and were edified by the Words that came forth. We knew the Lord was encouraging us with Rhema words that were for our situation. A few times the minister called either or both of us out from the audience and gave us personal prophecies about our situation indicating where the Lord was going to take us. We were comforted knowing that the Lord had orchestrated the whole situation we found ourselves in.

While in "the room," as we called it, we had to get out of ourselves more than ever and minister to other people. So, we decided to not look at our situation and focus on the Lord's work. The longer we were in "the room," I began to care less and less about what others thought about me. I understood that the Lord was not sharing with everyone what He was doing in my life. He was working on me so I could be useful to His Kingdom on another level.

The Lord was teaching me how to truly serve Him on His terms and not my own. This would take me, allowing the Lord to shape and mold my character even more. Prior to this purification process, I found it difficult to understand other people's struggles in Christ. There was so much the Lord needed to show me so that I would not look at other people with the wrong mindset or become self-righteous as so many leaders have become today.

I'll never forget the day I had made up my mind I was going to leave the room; I had been there about 8 months. I didn't tell anyone and didn't know where I was going to go. I left the room to run an errand and when I came back to get my things, I was met by a Prophetess that told me the Lord told her I was getting ready to leave, and if I did, I would miss my blessing. I didn't say a word. I knew to listen because no one knew of my plans except the Lord. She asked me if she could pray with me. As she was praying, she saw that I was going to be married soon, sooner than I thought. She also said that my blessing was right around the corner, "It is right at the door." Honestly, the work the Lord was doing in me was so deep, it was difficult not to bow under the pressure and stress, but the Lord sent help to make sure I was able to cooperate and accept what He was doing in my life. Once I yielded myself, things got better and a lot more peaceful.

We continued to focus on the souls the Lord placed in our path; we were actually having ministry for days and hours in that small room. It was packed out and the people continued to come. Yes, our situation was shameful and trying, but there were people hurting that needed our help. Although our ministry was in operation before we were evicted, we made sure not to draw anyone to ourselves. As we brought souls to the Lord, we prayed with them that the Lord would send them to a ministry where they could grow properly.

As we continued to fast and pray, the Lord put other people in our lives for us to bring to salvation. We didn't care who the people were, we just saw souls in need of salvation. We knew the Lord was with us because in one particular case, we were in a spiritual battle for souls that others felt were not worthy for the Lord to save. The battle was so strong that there was an assassination plot being planned for my future husband because of one of the souls the devil refused to release. The Lord fought on our behalf as we made late-night visits to their home; stayed up late praying and went on long fasts; believing God that the enemy would have to loose this soul. What people saw with their carnal eyes, we saw through spiritual eyes. This person had a great calling on their life and the enemy was fighting hard to make sure it was not fulfilled. We thank God that His power prevailed.

The blessed thing about these souls was they told us they desired for us to teach them. We didn't go after them; they came after us. Contrary to what others were saying, we were not trying to build a ministry to ourselves and my husband did not make himself an Apostle Prophet, nor did I make myself a Prophetess Evangelist. Anyone who knows Scriptures understands that the Lord chose us before the foundation of the world and He chose the appointed time to bring us forth and He did not need man's permission or approval. 2nd Timothy 1:9 declares, *"Who hath saved us, and called us with an holy calling, not according to our works, but according to his own purpose and grace, which was given us in Christ Jesus before the world began,"*

I'm surprised with how many people actually believe that Apostle Paul had hands laid on him to be ordained for ministry. Yes, they laid hands on him praying for his strength, but not to be ordained as an Apostle, Acts 13:2-4. The supernatural experience he had in seeing Jesus declared he was an Apostle and Acts 13:4 declares he was sent forth by the Holy Ghost. As soon as Saul was anointed, he went into the synagogues and preached Jesus, Acts 9:20. He didn't wait for a man's approval. Likewise, anyone who claims to be an Apostle today must have had a supernatural experience with Jesus of which my husband has had several by the power of the Holy Ghost.

While we were ministering and doing what the Lord told us to do, people were bad-mouthing us to other ministries who didn't know us. I know because some told us the things they heard. The funny thing was that I was not telling my family what was going on, so everything people heard was rumors and lies. We had "Christians" judging us based on rumors and lies. What a farce! I know at least one of the people running us down was a known hell raiser and the Church didn't know it. While they were pointing the finger at me, they couldn't even see the true nature of the person that was feeding them the lies. Why didn't these leaders hear from God concerning that? The Lord hid it from them according to 2nd Kings 4:27.

If you are a spiritual leader, be careful what you tell your congregation or people on your auxiliary about other people because what you are actually doing is launching a campaign against the Kingdom of God. Even Apostle Paul said in the book of Romans 10:2, *". . . they have a zeal of God, but not according to knowledge."* Especially if every time someone leaves a ministry to start a ministry or step out to do the will of God, you see them as a threat to your vision. You are not too high in God that the Lord cannot bring you down for spreading slanderous statements about His servants. O' Man, O' Woman, the Lord told me to ask you: Did you forget how you first started and how well-known spiritual leaders talked about you because they did not understand what the Lord was doing in your life? And now you have become likened to one of them that judged what the Lord was doing with you. Matthew 7:1-2 declares, *"Judge not, that ye be not judged. For with what judgement ye judge, ye shall be judged: and with what measure ye mete, it shall be measured to you again."*

Leader, consider what you are actually saying about people because some in your congregation will know the people you are slandering. They know that those you slander are not self-proclaimed and they know they have Christian character. For example, I was known by my family members and close Christian friends for a consecrated and sincere Christian lifestyle. It is said that people will believe a lie before they believe the truth. I'm not defending myself, but I desire to tell exactly what happened because someone reading this book may be going through the same thing. If you are being slandered, don't be concerned about what people are saying about you. If the Lord chose you, He will vindicate you. If you are the one doing the slandering, repent because judgment is coming.

On top of this, many of my family members were miserable comforters. They kicked me when I was down instead of praying for me. They jumped on the bandwagon and started talking about me and my situation. One thing in particular I noticed was, at a time when I needed my family to love me the most, they ran me down. Groups of them got together and talked about me instead of trying to make sure I was okay. They even put stipulations on me to keep in touch with them to prove my love to them. They made my situation about them!

I couldn't understand it; I was the one who needed a shoulder. I was the one who had helped them whenever they needed it, and now it was my turn and I felt knives between my shoulder blades.

The thing that gets me the most is, when you are in a Church, giving a lot of money and volunteering all of your spare time, they say you hear from God. However, when it is time to leave after many years of being faithful, so the Lord can use you in another vineyard and on another level because He has seen your faithfulness, suddenly you are a witch hearing from the devil. How can this be? I always hoped to leave this Church with my Pastor's approval and blessing, but things did not turn out that way for me because people were only concerned about their own vision and not the vision and will of God for my life.

I remember one time walking through the basement of the new house I purchased and the Lord said, "They're praying for you." I knew He was talking about the people in the Church I had just left. I said, "Lord, what are they praying?" He said, "That I open your eyes to the truth." I replied to the Lord, "Well, do it, show me the truth." I'm not afraid of the truth. The Lord answered those prayers and showed me a bunch of hypocrisy with the Church and in my natural family.

Everyone who said they had my best interest at heart was not really for me. He even showed me the truth about the man I was to marry. What He showed me about the people came through their behavior. It came through how they started to treat me. They revealed their true colors and turned their back on me when I was in need. They ran me down like a dog in the street and tried to sabotage my wedding ceremony. Someone, a so-called saint, even tried to stab my youngest son with a knife at a family event.

I will never forget a prophecy we received confirming that people who called themselves "Christians" were praying against us. These individuals were sending forth witchcraft prayers to bust up our relationship and hinder what the Lord was doing in our lives. They were actually praying that my divine connection would not marry me. On the one hand, we were fighting for new souls that we had brought to the Lord and on the other hand, we were fighting demonic attacks sent forth by these prayers. There were many times we would be in fasting and prayer and we would hear in the spirit realm what people were saying and praying against us. Most of our spiritual struggle was fighting the evil words people were trying to pray into our life.

Listen, just because someone doesn't agree with you, it does not mean they are an enemy of God. Even Apostle Paul said in 2nd Thessalonians 3:14-15, *"And if any man obey not the word of this epistle, note that man, and have no company with him, that he may be ashamed. Yet count him not as an enemy, but admonish him as a brother."* Me leaving the Church was not even a matter of doctrine. It was my time to go and for that, I was counted an enemy. Not one person in my family or at that ministry can lay anything to my charge, but they prayed against me. There are too many spiritual leaders abusing the authority the Lord has given them because they don't agree with or understand what the Lord is doing in His children's lives.

People were angry with us because we stepped out in faith and did what they were afraid to do for the Lord. So, they responded with backlash and took their own frustrations out on us. You will not believe how many Christians are waiting for man's approval to do what the Lord is telling them to do. **News flash!** By the time man gives you the approval to do what the Lord is telling you to do you will be old and decrepit. Look around. How many other people have your spiritual leader slandered when they stepped out to do the will of God? Eventually, if you get the courage to step out, it's going to happen to you too.

Many leaders are putting themselves in a dangerous place with God. Acts 5:27-28, 34, 38-39 declares, *"And when they had brought them, they set them before the council: and the high priest asked them, Saying, Did not we straitly command you that ye should not teach in this name? and behold, ye have filled Jerusalem with your doctrine, and intend to bring this man's blood upon us. Then Peter and the other apostles answered and said, We ought to obey God rather than men. . . . Then stood there up one in the council, a Pharisee, named Gamaliel, a doctor of the law, had in reputation among all the people, and commanded to put the apostles forth a little space; . . . And now I say unto you, Refrain from these men, and let them alone: for if this counsel or this work be of men, it will come to nought: But if it be of God, ye cannot overthrow it; lest haply ye be found even to fight against God."*

Even the people you're trying to get approval from have forgotten the time when the Lord told them to step out and do His will and everyone came against them. They have forgotten the moments of humiliation and embarrassment. They have forgotten the lies that were told and the pain the lies caused. They have forgotten those that were supposed to be for them that instead came out against them. They have also forgotten the tests and trials they had to go through to get the anointing they have.

After hearing the testimonies of other ministers, I soon learned that no matter how you leave a ministry that has a short-sighted or jealous spiritual leader, there may be a backlash from the Church, especially if the person leaving has been faithful to God and an asset to His Kingdom. Many ministers slander God's children when they leave in obedience to God; instead of following Gamaliel's council in the Book of Acts. The reason they say it's not God is because the Lord didn't tell them as the spiritual leader.

The Lord told me that He doesn't have to get man's permission when He is doing something. He didn't tell the Prophet Elisha when the woman of Shunem's son died, 2nd Kings 4:27; Apostle Peter didn't know the Lord was going to save the Gentiles, Acts 10:9-15; Joseph didn't know Mary was pregnant by the Holy Ghost, Matthew 1:19-20; and there are many, many more examples in the Bible. Listen, if you are a spiritual leader, be a spiritual leader; you are not God and He doesn't need your permission or approval for what He decides to do with His children. And if you have had a track record of messing over His servants in the past He can't trust you with this type of information, lest you prematurely give up the ghost and die in your sins.

Besides, if He told most of these spiritual leaders, they would be jealous and start to hinder God's plan because they never feel anyone is ready enough or they think someone is going to take some sheep with them. Who do the sheep belong to, you O' Man or God? Jesus said in Matthew 20:15-16, *"Is it not lawful for me to do what I will with mine own? Is thine eye evil, because I am good? So, the last shall be first, and the first last: for many be called, but few chosen."*

God is calling His children out of the four-walled Churches into the streets to get lost souls and the reason spiritual leaders are saying it's not God is because their eye is evil. They forgot they still had a lot of growing to do when the Lord chose them. Men in the Body of Christ are even being told they need a head before they can do the will of God. When Apostle Paul said in 1st Corinthians 11:3a-b, *"But I would have you know, that the head of every man is Christ;"*

it applied to ministry also. <u>Remember, I said in chapter 3, all this has to do with your divine connection and the work the Lord has for you both to do.</u>

Because we stepped out in faith to do the Lord's will, He was showing up on our behalf on a daily basis. Literally, He fed us daily. And if we didn't have food, we knew we were supposed to fast. It became a way of life, as if we were on the mission field, right here in America. The Lord also provided for us financially. I learned on a couple of occasions not to ask anyone for money because I lost the money that had been given to me by the time I got back to the room.

Where we lived, we had to pay by the week. There was no grace period. It took a lot of faith to stay in that place because we couldn't afford it. I remember one time when we were short $200 on our room bill. We had no idea where the money was going to come from. One Sunday, my future husband said the Lord instructed him to go visit a particular ministry. When he walked into the Church, he was asked to come up into the pulpit and share a couple of words of encouragement.

After he spoke, a woman met him coming out of the pulpit and handed him a folded sheet of paper. She said, "Apostle, the Lord

instructed me to give you this and that you should pray over me."
Going out the door he opened the paper and it was a check for $200.
When he came back to the room with the news, our faith leaped and
climbed to a new level. There were many signs like this that the Lord
was with us. We knew at this point we could trust the Lord for all our
needs. *"Trust in the Lord with all thine heart; and lean not unto thine
own understanding. In all thy ways acknowledge him, and he shall
direct thy paths" (Proverbs 3:5-6).*

Chapter 14

Finally, a Covering of My Own

"Now unto him that is able to do exceeding abundantly above all that we ask or think, according to the power that worketh in us, Unto him be glory in the church by Christ Jesus throughout all ages, world without end. Amen."

Ephesians 3:20-21

CHAPTER 14: FINALLY, a COVERING OF MY OWN

After all the drama, and three years and five months of, learning and growing, I finally married my divine connection, yeah!!!!! My wedding day was one of the many blessings the Lord has given me. Although we didn't have a lot of money, the Lord was moving on our behalf concerning everything from the dress to the venue.

I decided on my dress two years before we actually married. My eldest and most blessed sister picked it out. She saw it at the first bridal shop we went to. It was beautiful, and of course, I desired to keep looking at other shops only to come back to the original dress she chose. Well, the dress was $699 at the time and we had no money. So, I prayed that the Lord would hold the dress for me. After two years of not inquiring about the dress or placing a deposit on it, I went back into the shop in the spring prior to our wedding date to see if they still had it. It was there and marked down to $147. I was shocked and put it in the lay-away. My fiancé paid for it and the alterations. I was also able to purchase the perfect veil that matched the dress for $3. This is just one example of how the Lord moved on our behalf.

All the while the Lord was blessing us; some were working behind the scenes to sabotage our day. Many people returned the reply card to the invitation indicating that they would be attending the ceremony but were told not to come and did not let us know. Anyone who plans a wedding knows that the venue and catering are planned based on the number of people who have promised to attend, and payments are due in full prior to the event. I thank God He speaks to us and told us to only make plans for a certain number of people, which was two more than actually showed. Even people in my family changed their minds and did not come and didn't let us know. No matter what people tried to do to make it a disaster the day still turned out to be a beautiful event.

On my wedding day, I knew exactly who my family and friends were because they showed up. True family and friends stick by you when you need them the most. It is true, you know the people who really love you when you are down. They didn't have a lot of money or words to say to encourage me, yet they showed up and gave their support no matter what others were saying about us, and that went a long, long, long way. Now when people tell me they love me or miss me, I don't believe them if they didn't support me when I was down.

As a note, I am not advocating to leave your ministry to follow a man. You better know that the Lord is with you in your decision. And after you have made the decision understand if you are wrong you may have to live with it. It could be the death of you. One thing I am afraid of is being out of the will of God. I would not have left that ministry unless I fully believed the Lord was in it. That's the reason I left; I knew the Lord was in it! And yet, at times I wondered what life would have been like if I would have made a different decision.

So, eighteen months after my marriage, I earnestly began to pray and ask the Lord what would have happened if I would <u>NOT</u> have left the Church and followed the man who was to be my husband. When I had forgotten about the question, the Lord answered me a couple of days later. He showed me a dream where my family was in my life and we were all at an amusement park together as we had been in the past. I was still at the Church and was in love with a man who was a bus driver. We were not married, I was unsatisfied, and he was in love with me. I could feel his love in the dream. I was living with a family member at the time and was waiting for this man to come and pick me up for the evening. Everyone was pleased with me: the people in my family and the people at the Church.

Then suddenly in the dream, I saw myself running out of the house to meet him because he was coming to see me. As he came down the street, I saw him in a broken-down bus. The bus was barely making it down the street. The bumper and side panels were falling off. It was leaning on the driver's side as if it was going to fall over. The tires were flattened and the inside was full of trash. He had the biggest smile on his face and I saw his contentment. He was satisfied.

When I awoke, I was disturbed! I thought, "Lord, I'm happily married, why am I having this dream about another man?" When I began to pray concerning the dream, the Lord spoke to me and said, "This is the answer to your question." I said, "WOW! I would have ended up with a 'Broken down bus driver'." It was not about the type of job he had; it was his mediocrity that disturbed me. He was so lazy that he didn't even take the time to clean up the bus he was driving or to put in the service order for the repairs. Neither of us had an anointing nor vision for the future. We were going nowhere fast, and he was content with having nothing! I would have lost the gifts and the anointing the Lord had given me and I would have missed my calling! However, my family and the people in the ministry where I was were satisfied! After this, I stopped asking the Lord questions about what would have happened if I wouldn't have left.

This entire experience has shown me a lot of things. Mainly, that people make decisions they can't live with. Close family members of mine jumped on the bandwagon with the Church and chose not to have anything else to do with me. When the Lord calls His leaders out of the background, you will quickly realize whether the people around you really have true Christian character as they claim. In this book, I have mentioned many things that "Christians" were doing, but these were not "Christians" at all. The word Christian means "Christ-like;" the true "Christians" walk in holiness and they pray instead of getting caught up in a lot of mess.

The word declares in Luke 14:28-33 *"For which of you, intending to build a tower, sitteth not down first, and counteth the cost, whether he have sufficient to finish it? Lest haply, after he hath laid the foundation, and is not able to finish it, all that behold it begin to mock him, Saying, This man began to build, and was not able to finish. Or what king, going to make war against another king, sitteth not down first, and consulteth whether he be able with ten thousand to meet him that cometh against him with twenty thousand? Or else, while the other is yet a great way off, he sendeth an ambassage, and desireth conditions of peace. So likewise, whosoever he be of you that forsaketh not all that he hath, he cannot be my disciple."* If you are not willing to give up everything in this earth for the Lord, Jesus said you are not worthy to be His disciple.

That's why when all the chaos started to happen, I sat down at home alone to count up the cost of leaving the ministry. The things on my list actually happened and were harder to live with than the words I wrote on the paper. I make it a point to make decisions I can live with. I knew that my strength was going to only come from the Lord and I'm glad I trusted Him to keep me in that trial. My husband and I have survived a tough time in our relationship and we know that our marriage is not based on superficial fleshly emotions.

We know that we can make it through hard times as long as Christ is with us. The Lord placed some wonderful people in our life who were instrumental in encouraging us in our situation. Although it was only for a season, the Lord used them as catalysts to assist us in our spiritual deliverance. They prayed for us mightily because, again, we both had hurts and pains from past relationships that needed to be dealt with. After the Lord strengthened our relationship, I had to make a major personal decision to forgive all those who hurt me and to separate from them. The separation was necessary to maintain my deliverance and focus on what the Lord was calling me to do because the people you separate from will carry many of the spirits you have been delivered from. If you don't separate from them you will enter into a never-ending battle as long as you continue to allow them in your life. The Word declares in 2nd Corinthians 6:14, *"Be ye not unequally yoked together with unbelievers: for what fellowship hath righteousness with unrighteousness? And what communion hath light with darkness?"*

Before I left the Church, someone gave me some valuable counsel, "Don't invite anyone to your wedding who is not for you, your fiancé, or your union." I took this counsel a step further. Now, I don't allow anyone in my life that is not for the vision the Lord has given my husband and me. If someone doesn't believe in you and your vision for life, they will consciously or unconsciously be used by the devil to war against you and your vision. Amos 3:3 declares, *"Can two walk together, except they be agreed?"* This is not a Scripture only for married people. How can someone walk with you if you both are going in different directions? You can't, it's physically impossible.

Someone very dear to me once told me that she desired for me to be happy and she was glad that I finally got married. She remembered me talking about having a husband as a teenager. She knew it was one of my innermost desires and the Lord had fulfilled it. True love only comes once in a lifetime for most people and I'm finally enjoying it myself. Now, as it was prophesied to us, we have a very sweet marriage. We both adore and appreciate each other. We honestly can say we have a wonderfully satisfying marriage and now, I too can say I have a covering of my own.

It's Only the Beginning!

SPIRITUAL DISCLOSURE

Dear Reader,

As a Prophetess of the Lord Jesus Christ, I know that what I have experienced and written in this book was experienced and written for a special group of people that the Lord desires to bless. These are those that will be able to both understand and relate to what is written herein without being judgmental and/or critical. It has been written for those who have cried out to the Lord for strength because they have found themselves in some of the same situations that I have described in this book.

It is to you that I pray the Lord will strengthen you in your personal walk with Him as you wait on your divine connection. As you step out in obedience to the Lord against all opposition, I pray the Lord will direct every one of your steps and that he will enlarge your footsteps so that your feet will not slip. I pray that you will always be reminded that the Lord Jesus is the only one who can make what he has promised you come to pass. I pray you will have the patience and strength to wait for his promises. And even as Job's friends had to repent to him to appease the Lord's wrath from coming upon them, I pray that all your enemies will make peace with you and bring you gifts after the Lord has shut each and every one of their

mouths concerning you, in the name of the Lord Jesus Christ.

To all the doubters and haters that will judge and criticize the

experiences and revelation written in this book, I must warn you as

the Lord's Prophetess that you will be setting yourself up for the very

same things that you talk about to come upon you suddenly. That

which is ordained by the Lord no one can say anything against lest

they be thrust into that exact same situation. Romans 11:34 declares,

"For who hath known the mind of the Lord? Or who hath been his

counselor?" Just as they judged the Lord Jesus to their own

detriment, I realize that I will be judged by some who will be reading

this book to their own detriment. The Bible declares in Matthew

11:19 that <u>*WISDOM IS!*</u> justified of her children, *"The Son of man*

came eating and drinking, and they say Behold a man gluttonous, and

a winebibber, a friend of publicans and sinners. But wisdom is

justified of her children."

Proverbs 10:19 also declares, *"In the multitude of words there*

wanteth not sin: but he that refraineth his lips is wise." Therefore, be

wise and be silent concerning the things you do not agree with or

understand, for the Word of God declares, *". . . judge nothing before the time, until the Lord come, who both will bring to light the hidden things of darkness, and will make manifest the counsels of the hearts: and then shall every man have praise of God" (1ˢᵗ Corinthians 4:5).*

ABOUT THE AUTHOR

On July 12, 1996, I formally met the Lord Jesus Christ. Upon meeting Him, I confessed my sins and was baptized in water in the name of the Lord Jesus Christ. I committed my life to Him, and nine days later, I was filled with the Holy Ghost, receiving power from on High. He has been a blessing to me my whole life and has broken chains of oppression from off me. He has healed me mentally, physically, emotionally, and socially and has supplied all my needs. As of this day, I can say I lack nothing. He is and will forever be my King.

Furthermore, He has given me the strength to continue laboring beside my husband in ministry for over seventeen years. Although I serve in the capacities of Prophetess, Evangelist, Teacher, and Psalmist, I see myself as the Lord's handmaiden. The Lord has also given me the gift of authorship, charging me to write several books by the Holy Ghost's power and wisdom. He empowered me to earn four college degrees. The last is a terminal doctorate in Business Administration, with a Management Education specialization, from an accredited university. Everything I have accomplished has been by His power. All praises to Jesus Christ, King of Kings and Lord of Lords!

DISSERTATION

A quantitative study of selected predictors of job tenure, job satisfaction, and satisfaction with job promotion opportunity (2015)

BOOKS BY THE AUTHOR

1. The College Organizer Technique (E-book) (2009)
2. Are you really waiting: On God's promise for a divine spouse? (2010)
3. Understanding the Love of God in Church Hurt: It's Time to Heal! (2020, 2021)

CONTACT INFORMATION

Contact the author at *www.ATcicJMinistries.org*

CREDENTIALS

PhD, Capella University, Minneapolis, MN, Dec 2015
MSA, Central Michigan University, Mt. Pleasant, MI, Dec 2010
BBA, Eastern Michigan University, Ypsilanti, MI, Apr 2008
ABA, Oakland Community College, Bloomfield Hills, MI, Aug 2000

NOTES